CARDINAL NEWMAN
AND
WILLIAM FROUDE, F. R. S.

A Correspondence

CARDINAL NEWMAN

A pencil sketch by Miss Emmeline Deane

CARDINAL NEWMAN
AND
WILLIAM FROUDE, F.R.S.

A CORRESPONDENCE

BY
GORDON HUNTINGTON HARPER

WIPF & STOCK · Eugene, Oregon

Wipf and Stock Publishers
199 W 8th Ave, Suite 3
Eugene, OR 97401

Cardinal Newman and William Froude, F.R.S.
A Correspondence
By Harper, Gordon Huntington and Newman, John Henry
ISBN 13: 978-1-5326-7831-8
Publication date 12/24/2018
Previously published by The Johns Hopkins Press, 1933

TO
L. K. H.

PREFACE

THE following correspondence between Cardinal Newman and William Froude and his wife is largely unpublished hitherto. I am greatly indebted to the Oratorians of Edgbaston, Cardinal Newman's literary executors, for their permission to print these new letters, which were either in their files or in the possession of the Froude family. I wish particularly to record my thanks for the continued assistance and advice of Fr. Francis Bacchus, and for the hospitality of all the Oratorians while I was examining this correspondence. A few of the letters have before been published, and I have made due acknowledgment in my references. None of the letters of William Froude to Cardinal Newman has hitherto appeared in print, and for permission to give them here I am indebted to the daughter of William Froude, the late Baroness von Hügel, who generously devoted to me many hours of conversation about her family. It is through her kindness, also, that I am able to reproduce for the first time the pencil sketch of Cardinal Newman by Miss Emmeline Deane, which is the frontispiece of this book. I am equally indebted to Miss Mary Froude, who has answered my innumerable questions about her grandfather and permitted me to make the first publication of the letters Richard Hurrell Froude wrote to his brother in 1827 and 1828. These are given in the appendix.

In presenting this study of the relations of Cardinal Newman and William Froude I am indebted for advice and many helpful suggestions to Professor Raymond D. Havens of the Johns Hopkins University. Professor

George Boas also gave valued criticism, and Dr. Edward T. Norris, Dr. Edward N. Hooker, Dr. Arthur DuBois, and Dr. Archibald Hart gave of their time in helping to prepare this book for the press. To several friends at home and abroad I should like to acknowledge a debt of thanks none the less great because it is personal; of them all, none has been in everything more generous than T. L. H.

G. H. H.

THE JOHNS HOPKINS UNIVERSITY
December, 1933.

CONTENTS

CHAPTER		PAGE
I	INTRODUCTION	1
II	CORRESPONDENCE THROUGH 1845	33
III	CORRESPONDENCE THROUGH MARCH, 1857	71
IV	CORRESPONDENCE THROUGH JANUARY, 1860	109
V	CORRESPONDENCE THROUGH AUGUST, 1864	143
VI	FINAL CORRESPONDENCE	175
	APPENDIX	211
	INDEX	219

I
INTRODUCTION

I

INTRODUCTION

WHEN John Henry Newman was created Cardinal in 1879, he was an old and enfeebled man. His health was so seriously impaired after the trip to Rome for the conferring of the hat that it was more than once doubtful whether he would be able to take part in the ceremonies, but he managed, with St. Philip's help, to make all the addresses expected of him, replying to each presentation in words which only his genius could have put together. The effort, however, overtaxed his strength, and he had to forego many visits to the Pope and to the Holy Places of Rome. An affection of the lungs confined him to his rooms, and he was able only twice to say Mass even in the private chapel of his own residence.

However ill he might be, Newman felt that there was one task he could not put off for a single day. In the short time a curiously ironic fate had left to him, Newman desired to use his new position for the conversion of important thinkers to the Church, and the person above all others whom he wished most dearly to influence was one of the leading scientists of the day, Fellow of the Royal Society, freethinker, and lifelong friend, William Froude. For thirty-five years Newman had corresponded with Froude largely upon religious matters, endeavoring always to give the arguments for belief in the Roman Catholic Church in a fashion sufficiently cogent to win Froude over to that faith. Froude, however, remained unshaken in his scepticism, and in his replies pointed out to Newman the scientific objections which made such a step impossible for him. His letters were of great value to Newman in presenting the scientific point of view and had some small influence upon the development of Newman's thought up to the time when he set down his final statement in the *Grammar of Assent*. Although Newman recognized fully the difficulty of convincing Froude, he never despaired of final success, and his first sustained act, after his elevation to the Cardinalate, was to write, in spite of the danger to his health, a long letter, " a marvel of lucidity," in which he presented what he hoped was at last an irrefutable argument for the reasonableness of a belief in God. While he was correcting the rough draft of his argument, word came to him that William Froude was dead.

William Froude had had large claims upon Newman's friendship, for he was a brother of the " bright and beautiful " Hurrell who had helped to lead the Tractarians in their gallant and romantic attempt to save the English Church. Upon Hurrell's early death in 1836, William had succeeded in part to the place left empty in Newman's heart. Born at Dartington in 1810, he had grown up in unusual surroundings. His father, Archdeacon of Totnes, was typical of the more devout clergy of the eighteenth century. He had a lively interest in current affairs, in explorations, particularly those of Franklin, and was himself an artist accomplished enough to win praise from the dictator, Ruskin. He frequently gave to the Tractarians advice of a practical nature, and was himself enrolled as a member of that group. In the intellectual atmosphere of Dartington Parsonage, William and his younger brother, Anthony, lived during their most impressionable years, and here both of them heard the first plans for the

WILLIAM FROUDE

Oxford Movement discussed by Hurrell and his distinguished friends from the University, John Keble and John Henry Newman.

William's share of the Froude genius was sufficient at once to set him apart from his fellows when he went to Westminster School. His letters to Hurrel show him to have been a rather shy young man already more interested in mathematics than in football. Hurrell encouraged him to perfect himself in his studies, but cautioned him not entirely to neglect the more worldly matter of getting on with his companions and enjoying the benefits of competitive sport. In later life William often acknowledged the decisive influence his older brother had upon the formation of his mind. It was from Hurrell that he learned the principles of thinking which enabled him to win a distinguished place in the field of science. Hurrell's letters to him, some of which are given in the appendix, dealt not only with the necessity of right thinking but of right conduct. He advised him especially to distrust his emotions and the wild thoughts to which they could give rise. It will be not uninteresting to note, in the following correspondence, how fully William obeyed this caveat.

In 1828 William Froude entered Oriel College, Oxford, where he immediately drew attention to himself, so Hurrell wrote, by the depth of his science papers, which frequently overreached the abilities of the younger dons. Newman assisted in the direction of William's work, and during Hurrell's absences took upon himself the task of administering " periodical rowings " in classics and prose composition. In such hands it is small wonder that, throughout his life, William was able in his letters to reproduce to perfection the " Oriel style," and to win from his associates the tribute that of them all he best embodied the classic spirit.

When Froude went up to Oxford, Oriel was just beginning to assume the position, with Balliol, of the "prison house," and to its reputation for learning he contributed by his daily custom of rising at five-thirty to work steadily until two or three. He had at one time considered a medical career but shortly abandoned it for abstract science. Mathematics, in which he took a first, became his chief interest at the University, but he also dabbled in chemistry, and his rooms were made conspicuous in the court by the large stains of acid running from his windows down to the ground two floors below. His chief recreation was sailing, in which Hurrell had coached him, but even in this he turned his scientific bent toward the improvement of bows proper for racing craft.

In 1833 Froude took a position under Henry Robinson Palmer, vice-president of the Institute of Civil Engineers, and worked on the South Eastern Railway. Four years later he joined the engineering staff of Isambard K. Brunel, the designer of the *Great Eastern* steamship. While engaged in work on the Bristol and Exeter Railway, he made a contribution of major importance in propounding what is known to engineers as the "curve of adjustment." In the same year he married Miss Kate Holdsworth, and, in 1844, the two removed to Dartington to care for the aged Archdeacon, who was in failing health. Forced by this circumstance to relinquish his engineering career, Froude turned to experimental science. In 1856 he was asked by Brunel to make some investigations of the motion of ships in waves. This study became the major work of his lifetime and gained for him a place in the first rank of British scientists. His experiments were carried on

WILLIAM FROUDE

privately in the estuaries about Salcombe, and Froude was frequently seen by the natives rowing about apparently playing with toy boats. When on one occasion two uniformed men (naval officers interested in the experiments) were seen at the oars, a story spread about the locality that William Froude was mad and had to be in charge of two "keepers." By 1868 his work had so far progressed that he made formal application to the Chief Constructor of the Navy, Sir Edward James Reed, for the building of a covered experimental tank suitable for testing model ships. His proposals were approved by the Admiralty on February 1, 1870, and the tank was constructed. Froude developed a mechanism whereby models in wax could be cut directly from the plans of the proposed vessel. He also determined a "law of similitude and comparison" whereby, from the results of tests upon the model, he was able to make extraordinarily accurate predictions concerning the behaviour of a full-sized ship.

Froude's development of the experimental tank profoundly affected the course of all naval designing. Out of this work grew his invention of a bilge keel able to hold vessels more steady in wave action. His results were at once applied to British warships and subsequently to the commercial ships of every country. The British Government only recently completed an elaborate tank, dedicated by Stanley Baldwin in November, 1932, as the *William Froude Laboratory*, a part of the new National Physical Laboratory at Teddington. "Today there are more than a score of experimental tanks in existence," Mr. Baldwin said in his speech, "and everyone of them is a monument to the genius and work of Froude."[1] The first purely com-

---

[1] *Nature* (Nov. 26, 1932), p. 801.

mercial tank built in England in 1881 bore an inscription to William Froude as "the greatest of experimenters and investigators in hydrodynamics."

The Royal Society elected Froude to membership on June 2, 1870, and in 1876 awarded him their Gold Medal. Froude contributed a number of papers to the publications of the Royal Society as well as several to the Institute of Naval Architects.

It is not, however, Froude's scientific career which is of concern here, but rather his private life, particularly as it related to John Henry Newman. That life was a less than ordinarily happy one, and to the unhappiness Newman largely contributed. A close friend not only of William's but also of Mrs. Froude's, Newman corresponded regularly with them, and the topic most frequently discussed was not unnaturally religion. While Newman remained an Anglican his long letters to the Froudes dealt with his position in that faith, and some of them, as will be seen, were of a most intimate nature. After he became a Roman Catholic, Newman introduced into his letters a subtle proselytizing which was not without effect. First one and then another of the Froude family were converted by Newman's influence to Catholicism, until finally William alone remained a Protestant, spiritually isolated from his family. During these years Froude carried on with Newman something of a philosophical inquiry into the nature of the evidence for religious belief.

Mrs. Froude was the first to be converted. She confessed her faith on March 19, 1857. Her action was a great blow both to William and to Archdeacon Froude, who threatened to cut his son out of the inheritance of his considerable fortune, saying he would not leave his property to Catholics. William offered to resign his place at Dartington in favor of Anthony and to return to his engineering career. But Anthony's militant agnosticism was even more unacceptable than Mrs. Froude's Catholicism, and in the end William inherited the entire estate of £35,000. To Newman's constant influence was now added that of Mrs. Froude, and eventually four children became Catholics, and one of them, Robert Edmund, for a time considered entering the priesthood.

Froude bore his spiritual trials most patiently, never allowing his feeling of isolation to impair his love for his wife and family. He continued to discuss frankly and openly religious questions and their relation to scientific thought. He appreciated the beauty of the Anglican church service and knew from memory many of the poems of the *Christian Year*. In the family circle he read the Bible in a spirit at once sympathetic and understanding, seeking out always the depth of meaning in the most beautiful passages. Upon the birth of his first daughter he had given to the parish church a memorial window. When in later years there was left to him only one child, Mary, who was not a Catholic, he engaged for her a Protestant governess. Even this last spiritual consolation was lost to him upon the child's death in 1863.

Archdeacon Froude died in 1859, and the Froudes moved to Torbay and later built a house, Chelston Cross, near Torquay. Here a brilliant society, English, French, and American, often gathered. Arnold, Jowett, Ruskin, and Brunel were frequent guests. To William Froude foreign governments sent representatives, among them Popoff of the Czar's navy, for consultation on matters of naval design. Froude was a member of the Athenaeum Club, and by reason of his personal charm and intellectual distinction a popular figure in London society.

In spite of his softness of personal manner, Froude never relinquished his " tough-minded " attitude, and to the end of his life he remained firmly agnostic, sceptical even of the possibility of absolute certainty in secular as well as religious matters. The intimate contact of Newman and Froude, the one passionately believing and the other fiercely sceptical, the influence of one upon the other, and their personal relationship form the subject of the following correspondence.

Mrs. Froude died in 1878, and that winter, Froude, who suffered greatly by the loss, accepted the invitation of the Government to cruise to South Africa on the *Boadicea*. As he was preparing to return to England, he was taken suddenly ill and died at Simon's Town June 4, 1879. He was buried in the military cemetery with full honors on June 12.

Froude's sincere and devoted friendship had been invaluable to Newman. Bound by such close ties of personal affection, Newman felt free to talk to Froude as he could to no other of his friends who were not Catholics. Enjoying such intimacy and appreciating fully the intellectual acumen of his former pupil, Newman found in Froude one with whom he could discuss problems of religious belief which were either unknown to or beyond the grasp of his own circle. Froude was an outstanding thinker in the particular field wherein lay the greatest danger to Catholicism, and from Froude Newman gained a wealth of information and a new viewpoint which served him well in solving the difficulties presented to himself and other Catholics by their beliefs.

Froude may be said in a measure to have served Newman as a testing block upon which to beat out a solution to some of his difficulties, and evidences of Froude's criticism may be found in the *Grammar of Assent*. Froude was of so much assistance to Newman in attempting to solve intellectual problems largely from the very fact that his cast of mind was very different from Newman's. He always believed that he had developed legitimately the principles of thinking Hurrell had instilled in him, and when later he became a complete sceptic, it was, he said, because his thinking had been so largely in the domain of " practical science, where, more than elsewhere, the principles and results of reasonings are confronted with the test of direct experiment." [2] And when as often as not the results of his careful thinking suffered correction from still further investigation, it is not astonishing that he came to believe the establishment of any permanent truths a fruitless endeavor. Repeated experiences had made him reluctant to accept any proposition not supported by overwhelming evidence of the most practical sort, and even in those cases where he seemed to have arrived at certainty, Froude allowed always for the possibility that the ultimate assumption, small or axiomatic though it might be, upon which every argument rested, was itself wrong. From continued application to problems of a practical nature Froude drew two related rules for his thinking: there is a moral obligation to doubt every proposition and conclusion; the achievement of permanent certainty is impossible. In his own words, " Our ' doubts ' in fact appear to me as sacred, . . . more strongly than I believe anything else I believe this— that on no subject whatever, distinctly not in the region

[2] December 29, 1859.

of the ordinary facts with which our daily experience is consonant, distinctly not in the domain of history or of politics, and yet again *a fortiori* not in that of Theology, is my mind (or as far as I can take the mind of any human being), capable of arriving at an absolutely certain conclusion." [3]

With such intellectual principles Froude was unable to accept orthodox religious tenets, and in this inability he was representative of a large class of serious thinkers. His arguments against existing creeds, being susceptible of a high degree of demonstration, carried a corresponding preponderance of conviction among those who faced squarely the problem of religious belief. As a scientist interested in reaching the truth, whether in physical or metaphysical questions, he was a distinguished exemplar of that tough-minded school of philosophical liberalism against which Newman spent a life in combat.

Yet in personal relationship Newman did not find Froude tough-minded, but, on the contrary, a sincere and kindly critic of orthodoxy whose great desire was not so much to destroy accepted opinion as it was to establish as far as possible a truth against which no force of untruth could prevail. If he held liberal views, he held them only as a result of a patient sifting of the evidence which produced them. His zeal for repeated correction and his sceptical attitude were a source of some confusion to Newman, who held that only minds religiously disposed were capable of discovering religious truth. Sincerity of purpose was to Newman indispensable in a seeker. Although Newman did not find Froude naturally religious, he did recognize in him a sincere desire to discover whatever truth there was in

[3] *Ibid.*

religion. He saw in him neither a rude scoffer nor an iconoclast, but an English gentleman (and the gentleman counted much with Newman) who for some reason could not convince himself of the truth of religion. Since the fault did not lie with Froude's sincerity nor entirely with the disposition of his mind, Newman was forced to believe that it lay with the state of Christian apologetic, and he set about discovering some polemical means for overcoming Froude's intellectual difficulties. The task was all the more congenial since Froude himself enjoyed serving as a target for the arrows of Newman's dialectic by which they both hoped to solve the great problem presented in the nineteenth century by the clash of religion and science.

It was, therefore, much in the spirit of philosophical inquiry that during the years between 1838 and 1844 Newman and Froude had a number of conversations on religious topics which they frequently continued by letter. Newman seems for a time to have regarded their inquiry in the old relationship of tutor and pupil, and he occasionally had some fears that his younger friend might be " unsettled," a feeling he himself appreciated only too keenly. Newman did not have the same hesitation in outlining his thoughts to Mrs. Froude, whose cast of mind was more disposed toward religious belief, for she had repeatedly urged him to write to her on such matters. Hence the practice grew up of including her in the correspondence, Newman intending that she should always show his letters to her husband.

No conclusions seem to have been drawn immediately; rather, the question became, for Newman at least, yearly more complicated. His intellectual progress from 1838 to the writing of Tract 90 in 1841 is too well known to review here. From 1841 to 1845

Newman was only waiting for the decision which could not have come sooner than it did. The state of his mind was suspected by many of his friends, and it was commonly thought that soon he would " go over ". Nevertheless, no one dared intrude questions upon him until at last Mrs. Froude, in July, 1843, was so bold as to write asking directly whether or not he was contemplating a change to Rome in the very near future. To her question Newman replied:

Littlemore.
July 28, 1843.

My dear Mrs. Froude,

I wish I could write you such an answer to your letter as it deserves. I mean a real open letter, saying first what I think, but I feel it so difficult to bring out what I would say, that when I attempt it, I become unreal. One difficulty is the analysing and knowing one's feelings—but another is to be able to exhibit them on occasion. I do not carry them in my hand, and, much as I wish it, I cannot put you in possession of them on the mere asking.

There is no doubt at all that I am approximating towards Rome; not any doubt that those who are very much about me see this little as I wish it. These two facts, coupled with the very significant and corresponding fact of the Bishops, Heads of religious parties, and organs of religious opinion having disowned me, have determined me on resigning St. Mary's, though as yet I have not made this known, nor shall I till the time comes. I feel I am no longer able to fulfil such a *trust*, as a pastoral charge in our Church implies; and, as on the whole I have hitherto ever been aiming at obeying and supporting her rulers, to the best of my ability, so, when I can no longer do this, and especially when they refuse my assistance, it seems a call upon me to release myself from the obligation. As time has gone on, I have become more dissatisfied with the established system, and *its conductors* have become more dissatisfied with me; I do not see what good can come of continuing a relation, which each party wishes brought to an end.

If I were ever so sure of continuing just in my present state of mind, these considerations would tell—but it is obvious that, taking circumstances as they are, I may get into serious difficulties if I continue to hesitate about a step which has already employed my mind for three years.

Speaking candidly with you I will say that I do not see beyond this. I shall retire from St. Mary's, if nothing happens, as quietly as I can, and then shall remain here, with pretty much the same occupations as I have at present. Alas! there is something very awful in putting an end to duties which have lain upon me now for 16 years nearly, and, as it were, making up a book which will not be opened till another world. And if you had any idea how miserably those duties have been fulfilled by me, you would partly enter into my feelings on losing all opportunity of retrieving them.

As to the future, I think that of one thing every one may be quite certain, as far as I dare promise anything of myself, that I should do nothing sudden, or without people in general being prepared for it. It may be the will of Providence to leave me just where I am, or to lead me on further. His guidance is commonly slow. Quick movements offend people, as for other reasons, so because they are unlike the effects of a heavenly guidance. And they shock, unsettle, and distress them besides.

Now, my dear Mrs. Froude, this will seem to you a very cool letter, but you asked a very cool question and as you are about the only person who has so asked, you are the only person who has been so answered.

Let us not take thought for the morrow, but be content with what is put before us for the day present. *You* feel this quite, as your letter shows. I was very sorry my talk with William was interrupted. I had long wished for one, yet dreaded it; dreaded it, because it is not pleasant to be running the risk of unsettling a person. And though I know well he is of far too manly a merit to be swayed by another in such a matter, yet I might be suggesting objections to him in the course of our conversation which would afterwards hang about him and trouble him. I have had no hesitation of writing freely to you, because you have anticipated me.

Ever yrs affectionately,
John H. Newman.

So particular was the claim of the Froudes upon him that Newman found it only natural, once he had made a beginning, to keep them informed of his progress toward Rome. By April, 1844, he felt the change to be imminent, and so he opened fully to Froude " a subject which I have long wished to write to you about . . . and felt myself quite cruel toward you and your wife not to do so." There followed, then, at intervals of a few days, the series of long letters which make up the following chapter of this book. Newman described all the difficulties which were besetting him in these letters, and they may be thought of therefore as a contemporary " apologia " which is all the more valuable from having been written during the days of strain and not recollected in the comparative tranquillity of twenty years later.

For Newman the letters were a catharsis of his religious doubts and emotions. His ostensible reason for writing was to give such an account of himself as might at the same time answer a question Froude had put to him. " I am in great perplexity to know what to do about my letters," he wrote Mrs. Froude, " I began with a view of relieving a difficulty of William's, not of urging arguments against our existing position. But in my last letter I was betrayed into doing so." [4] But after he had begun to discover to the Froudes the intimate work-

[4] April 12, 1844.

ings of his mind, he persevered to a conclusion, not so much for their sakes as for the benefit to himself. " Since my object in writing," Newman explained, " has ceased to be that with which I began (viz. that of removing a painful feeling which William seemed to have) . . . I have become very anxious about the effect of my letters upon you . . . *for I am not writing with a purpose so much as finishing a subject I may not otherwise get myself to work out.*" [5]

The change in attitude that came over Newman marked the first occasion of real importance where he used Froude as an anvil upon which to beat out the solutions to his own pressing problems. Within a few years purely personal considerations were to make Froude a much more critical person upon whom to test philosophical arguments.

On October 8, 1845, to the regret and often to the horror of the many friends who looked to him as their spiritual adviser, Newman made his general confession of faith in the Roman Catholic Church. If his defection was a serious blow to Anglicanism, it was the personal repercussions upon his friends that gave Newman most concern. He felt at times like a lost leader, and the pain of separating from Oxford was with him to the day of his death. Many of his friends he did not see again for years, and many he never saw again. The breaking of such intimate ties of association brought a loneliness which there were few friends to assuage, but among the few Protestants who still loved him and sympathized with him, none was more understanding than William Froude. If at this time Newman was more widely separated from him on philosophical

---

[5] *Ibid.* Italics mine.

grounds, he was certainly not so in affectionate regard, and Froude's very kindness made Newman rely the more heavily upon him for advice in approaching the troublesome problems which were presenting themselves. To whatever question he might pose, Newman received a criticism which, while he desired it to be penetrating and impartial, he was none the less grateful for its having been given always in the most courteous of terms. And so, after 1845, the correspondence between Newman and the Froudes (often addressed to Mrs. Froude) continued as before upon its philosophical course.

Within a few years, however, a circumstance arose which severely tried Froude's impartiality and at the same time directed with greater intensity his whole acumen to a consideration of the problem of the rational basis for a belief in Roman Catholicism. This circumstance was Newman's proselytizing of Mrs. Froude. Newman was not a professional proselytizer, like Manning, gauging his usefulness by the number and prominence of his converts. He urged Catholicism upon Mrs. Froude as one would urge knowledge upon the ignorant; he felt that he possessed the secret of eternal blessedness, and he wished to share it with those he loved most dearly. Froude protested against what seemed to him the unfairness in attempting deliberately to influence a mind naturally biased by temperament toward Catholicism. He felt that Newman did not recognize the highly dubious nature of the evidence for Catholicism, and thus to Froude, who held passionately to the uncertainty of everything, Newman's dogmatizing was actually painful. While Froude heartily encouraged intellectual inquiry, whether into Catholicism or any other problem, he maintained that inquiry should be free from personal persuasion. He felt that Newman was rather exceeding the bounds of disinterested investigation when he began to urge upon Mrs. Froude the particular points of Catholic belief most likely to appeal to her sympathetic mind. He protested the situation to Newman, who at once acknowledged the error of his zeal. " Your dear wife," he wrote in reply, " has said she would not write to me again—and I assure you, my dearest William, I shall not write to her—but you can't hinder me (nor wish to hinder me) praying, whatever prayers are worth." [6]

Nevertheless, Newman did not cease to write to Mrs. Froude letters presenting the claims of the Catholic faith, and Mrs. Froude herself finally pointed out to Newman the awkward situation his letters caused. But considerations of worldly delicacy weighed little against Newman's desire to put before her in a true light the blessings of Catholicism, and it was not a month before he wrote her, " Do not fancy you can put me in a painful position to dear William, I don't mind differing with him. I don't mind giving you advice in which he would not concur. But I wish to be sure I tell him when I do it. He is so true and tender, but I leave you safely to him. But I can never disguise from him what I think and feel about you." [7]

Newman might here appear in a bad light were it not that he believed completely in the truth of what he urged, and Froude acknowledged his sincerity and honesty of purpose. While Froude felt that Newman was presenting the case one-sidedly, he also realized that it did not appear so to Newman. And Newman, not unaware of the delicacy of the situation, was

[6] April 10, 1854.   [7] May 5, 1854.

nevertheless willing to suffer some unpleasantness in his desire to confer eternal benefit upon his friends. Throughout his correspondence Newman never wrote to make cheap points but endeavored always to put forth his arguments straightforwardly, allowing them to stand as much as possible upon their merits. He sought to understand the perplexities of his friends and to make sympathetic suggestions which might not readily occur to an uneasy mind. Both the Froudes were aware of Newman's real motive in writing and appreciated his desire to share with them a truth which seemed to him to be temporarily hidden from their eyes. Because he understood Newman's pious motive and because he shared in his zeal for truth, Froude did not forbid the continuation of Newman's correspondence with his wife; rather, he entered upon it himself.

Froude entered this particular phase of the correspondence for a single reason, to present opposite arguments in an attempt to arrive at the truth which he felt lay somewhere between Newman and himself. What had before amounted to a disinterested argument upon a metaphysical question now had added to it the incentive of personal moment. Holding intellectual honesty above every other ideal, Froude could but be immeasurably distressed by his wife's leanings toward Catholicism, for to him the whole Catholic argument appeared but a tissue of supposition; there was no single proposition that did not seem to him insecurely based or unsupported by practical evidence. Consequently it was with real anguish that Froude saw one dear to himself foregoing every claim to rationalism and accepting a philosophy logical enough within itself but incapable of verification and therefore to him essentially unacceptable.

WILLIAM FROUDE

With the succeeding years Froude found himself more and more actively opposed to Newman's thinking, and their correspondence in the following chapters will be seen to take on the color of a philosophical battle. In so far as there was a material victory, it lay with Newman, for to Froude's deep distress his wife joined the Catholic Church in 1857, and within a few years she was followed by her two sons, Hurrell and Edmund. The additional loss of his sons was to Froude almost insupportable, particularly that of Edmund, who had begun to display distinct signs of the Froude genius for science.

Despite his personal interest which urged him to present only arguments telling against religious belief, such was the impartiality of Froude's mind that he was as concerned to arrive at some solution of the problem as he was to prevent by argument Mrs. Froude's relinquishing her intellectual integrity. He displayed to an amazing degree the truly philosophic cast of mind which enabled him to regard dispassionately a problem which was at the same time of vital personal consequence. His genius bore the characteristic stamp of humility. It was not his wish ruthlessly to destroy religious belief. He had from youth an innate sympathy with the Anglican Church in which he had grown up, and all his life he retained a love for the beauty it fostered, but he would have truth in that beauty, and it was with the purpose to discover as far as possible the truth that Froude continued to correspond with Newman. He felt throughout that if Newman were able to establish the certainty of Roman Catholicism, he need then have no slightest regret over his wife's professing that faith; indeed, in that case, he was prepared himself to accept it with only the single reservation that he might give it up immediately in the event that a preponderance of new evidence should be at any time be brought against it.

Froude desired that his opponent's arguments should enjoy the same degree of elucidation he attempted to secure for his own, and hence there grew up the paradoxical situation of Froude's suggesting upon several occasions arguments which he felt Newman might possibly be able to make tell against the very tenets he held most dear. And hence it was, too, that Froude, on behalf not only of himself but of men of science generally, urged Newman really and fully to work out his argument for the reasonableness of a belief in God. It was Froude's correspondence which served in part as an incentive for Newman to do what he might not have done without this urging, and that was to marshal his thoughts for an extended answer to a problem so immense as that of the grounds for religious belief. In replying to one letter in which Froude had outlined considerations he thought important, Newman wrote, " The line you draw out in your letter is familiar to me and I don't even know when I first began to feel it, not that you do not bring it out more clearly than I perhaps have done to myself. *I will keep your letter before me to use.* Still I have long meditated on its subject. I think it a fallacy . . . but I don't think it easy to show it to be so. It is one of various points I have steadily set before me as requiring an answer and an answer from me." [8]

When the *Apologia* appeared four years later, it did something toward answering the question, but it did not directly attack the broad problem underlying the difficulty of attaining by reasonable means a belief in

---

[8] January 2, 1860. Italics mine.

God. It gave an extraordinary view of the logical and psychological considerations which had weighed with a single man in accepting the Roman Catholic faith, but as an apologetic it was scarcely applicable to the needs of the many. When, therefore, within a few weeks there appeared in *Fraser's Magazine,* of which Anthony Froude was then editor, an article by Fitzjames Stephen, " Dr. Newman's Apologia ", in which the idea of " probability as the guide of life " was touched on, Froude thought it opened to Newman an opportunity for rebutting the scientific critics as crushingly as he had Kingsley. He wrote calling Newman's attention to the article and expressing the hope that he would answer it, first because it stated the sceptical case so succinctly, and then because " the counter view which so entirely satisfies you must be capable of very powerful and very clear justification, and you are of all men the one to undertake the exposition of this." [9]

What Froude really urged was that Newman write the book which ultimately appeared as the *Grammar of Assent.* It was late in the day, Newman felt, to begin so strenuous a task, and he had many misgivings in spite of the feeling that not yet had he exerted that influence over men's minds which had been for years his great ambition. Newman was sixty-four years old, and so far every great endeavor of his had been brought to an inglorious conclusion through the interference of his superiors; his work in the Oxford Movement, his plans for the Irish University and for Catholic education in Oxford had been set at naught by Protestants and Catholics alike. He had begun to think of himself as a *miles emeritus* and not as one girding himself for so

---

[9] October 8, 1864. The idea of " probability " (found in Pascal) was by no means new in the Church.

severe an encounter as this promised to be. Nevertheless he did begin tentatively to outline to Froude the probable course his thought would take. He concluded his letter with words which show something of his reliance upon Froude's generous and kindly criticism, " I have many trials and discouragements in the midst of enormous mercies, but should I be led to pursue the subject of this letter (which would be by very slow marches) *I should ask your leave to put various points before you,* as iron girders are sent to the trying house." [10]

It was six years before Newman finally gave to the problem of reasonable religious belief the solution which had been developing in his mind since the delivery of his *University Sermons*. The thinking in the *Grammar of Assent* had its roots in the lecture halls of Oxford where Newman had first read Butler's *Analogy,* a book which perhaps more strongly than any other had influenced a generation of Oxford men. Hurrell Froude too had drawn much of his intellectual inspiration from it, and in their official capacity as tutors at Oriel both of them had so implanted in William the dictum of Butler's that probability is the guide of life that it formed the permanent basis of his later thought. From this common point William Froude and Newman had set out upon different courses and travelled always further apart; and yet a careful examination of the progress of each one would probably reveal no error in logic, proving what Newman had always maintained, that from a single source two logical minds might nevertheless diverge.

Newman's philosophical creed in regard to religious belief relegated reason (by which he meant, with

[10] January 18, 1860. Italics mine.

Coleridge, the *Verstand*, the power of proceeding logically in intellectual matters) to a place secondary to faith, which in his conception amounted to a kind of super-reason not unlike Coleridge's conception of the *Vernunft*. A fundamental point of his belief was that one attains religious truth differently from the way one arrives at the truth in secular matters. In the latter field conclusions are drawn solely by the logical reasoning faculty, the *Verstand*, and one accepts as true that side of a question having the preponderance of evidence or of probabilities in its favor. But for arriving at the truths of religion, Newman believed that a different technic was necessary from the fact that the reason which operated on the natural phenomena of the material world was incapable of transcending to the realm of the supernatural. For attaining supernatural truths a particular disposition or quality of mind was indispensable. To a simply reasoning mind, relying only on the *Verstand*, a portion of the evidence concerning supernatural phenomena was imperceptible; only the super-reasoning faculty of the mind could apprehend it. Hence, only to the religiously disposed were the truths of religion possible.

Newman apprehended the existence of God through conscience and through the analogy of the natural and the revealed constitution of the world. His concern was not to prove the existence of God but only to establish a means for the ordinary man to believe reasonably in His existence. His effort, therefore, was directed to discovering and developing arguments of such a reasonable nature that the ordinary man could without hesitation give whole-hearted assent to them and thereupon attain to that comfortable state of certitude from which he need have no slightest doubt that he would ever be shaken. Newman analyzed the psychological and logical processes involved in giving to arguments the assent which produces a state of certitude. He distinguished two kinds of assent, notional and real; notional assent being assent to an idea, real to a thing. "In its notional assents as well as in its inferences," Newman wrote in the *Grammar of Assent,* "the mind contemplates its own creations instead of things; in real, it is directed toward things, represented by the impressions which they have left on the imagination."[11] The change from notional to real assent is like that from theory to practice. "It will sometimes happen," Newman said, in illustrating this point, "that those who acquitted themselves but poorly in class, when they come into the action of life, and engage in some particular work, which they have already been learning in its theory and with little promise of proficiency, are suddenly found to have what is called an eye for that work—an eye for trade matters, or for engineering, or a special taste for literature—which no one expected from them at school, while they were engaged on notions."[12] Our nature is so constituted that we assent more readily to things than to ideas, and this real assent alone produces a state of certitude which is indefectible. Our notional assents are naturally less convincing. With this distinction made, Newman's problem was then to show that one may bridge the gap from notional to real assent to the idea of God's existence and arrive at the consequent state of certitude.

In bridging this gap Newman relied upon a fact of

---

[11] *Grammar of Assent* (London, 1924), p. 75.
[12] *Ibid.,* pp. 75-76.

human experience which led him to believe that the primary sources of our assent are not logical but go back to our emotional and practical nature. Upon occasion we "think with our whole being" and arrive at truths of which we should have been incapable by the use of only the logical reasoning faculty (*Verstand*). "All men have a reason," said Newman, "but not all men can give a reason." A favorite illustration of his was of the weather-wise farmer predicting rain when every perceptible sign pointed to a clear day. He pointed out that geniuses have often been noted for this ability to overgo the merely logical faculty of the mind and arrive in a flash at the truth. It was by such flashes that Napoleon could with a glance take in the disposition of enemy forces and have immediately a counter-plan in mind. In mathematics Newton had had the same sort of intuition. Newman's whole argument depended upon the validity of this instinctive ability to arrive at right conclusions through the "accumulative force of a multitude of reasons which if taken singly were only probabilities." To this instinctive faculty he gave the name of the illative sense.

It was about the potentiality of the illative sense that much of Newman's correspondence with Froude revolved. Faced with the problem of demonstrating to a practical scientist a practical means for accepting a belief in God, Newman had of necessity to use arguments of a practical sort, and he singled out this particular psychological experience because its existence was universally recognized. If, then, he could also establish its validity among a generality of thinking men, he felt the problem would be satisfactorily solved. Newman had for a long time been working toward this conclusion, that in the illative sense lay the means of establishing his case, but he had not so far developed it in words. When finally in 1864 he realized the all-importance of this particular point, it must have been with some trepidation that he specifically propounded it to Froude for his criticism as, in his own words, "iron girders are sent to the trying house." On no other occasion had he submitted a problem of such vital importance. He had before availed himself freely of Froude's criticism, both in conversation and by letter, to sharpen ideas which were not entirely clear in his own mind, but he had not outlined anything of such vital importance. Newman felt that if Froude could be made to admit that the manner of attacking secular matters differed from that of religious matters and also that the make-up of the mind was itself the ruling factor in arriving at the truth in questions concerning the supernatural, then he might himself the more confidently rely upon the argument which had satisfied one so sceptical.

Froude's answer was sufficiently in agreement to imbue Newman with confidence, for in his reply he used the very words Newman felt most pertinent to the question. "At least it seems to be," Froude said in giving the assurance Newman so much desired, "a tenable view, a priori, that men are intended to deal differently with their conclusions when these lead up into Religion from that way in which they deal with conclusions relating to the ordinary affairs of life . . . as if instinct were to guide them in one case, logic in the other . . . if the distinction is regarded as sound, it seems at once necessary to assume that men are gifted with an instinctive faculty which enables them to perceive with certainty the facts of a supernatural occurrence, and to recognize it as supernatural at once and by a conscious act of unerring recognition instead of by intricate (and to a man of science impossible) process of determining in the first place that it is not natural." [13]

Newman chose to accept Froude's letter as entirely sanctioning the argument submitted to him, and he proceeded to develop his thought in that direction in the *Grammar of Assent.* His argument when finished was imperfect, and Newman was not unaware of it. There remained always objections unanswered, but Newman felt that he was at least on the right track and that such imperfections as existed arose rather from faulty execution than from mistaken premises.

Froude recognized at least the possibility of Newman's being rightly directed, but he had not meant to offer all the encouragement Newman chose to believe. He had worded his reply carefully, and while he thought Newman's distinguishing between technics as applied to secular and religious questions was a "tenable view," a priori, he added that an "abundant crop of intractable difficulties arise when one attempts to reduce the distinction into a rule of practical application." Moreover he felt most sceptical about the possibility of the human mind's immediately and unerringly recognizing a supernatural event, because, he said, it was "extremely difficult if not impossible to draw a clear and available line between the probabilities which lead up to religion and those which belong to common life so interwoven the two classes of question are when one really looks into them." [14]

Newman set about overcoming these intractable difficulties. His attempt, brilliant though it was as an intellectual *tour de force,* was largely unsuccessful. His

[13] October 8, 1864.   [14] *Ibid.*

reliance upon instinctive thinking, thinking with one's whole being (therefore partly with the emotions), made a primary consideration the natural make-up of the person doing the thinking. Thus the very human tendency to believe what is most congenial received from Newman a whole-hearted sanction where a cautious analysis would have been more consistent with the spirit of philosophical inquiry. Reduced to its simplest terms, Newman's argument approached dangerously near the proposition that belief produced truth. "*We can believe what we choose*," Newman wrote in 1847, "We are answerable for what we choose to believe." [15] Consequently one to whom religious thinking was congenial could with small difficulty arrive at a certainty personally satisfying in matters of religion, and anyone who by reason of temperament found it impossible to arrive at such certitude had only to exercise the "will" and induce a more sympathetic attitude, whereupon a perception of the truth of religion (and of the Roman Catholic faith) would naturally follow.

In spending so much of the force of his argument on analyzing the illative sense Newman did not sufficiently attend to defining or analyzing the "right state of mind" which alone instinctively found the truth. Newman himself arrived at what he believed to be the truth by giving free play to his natural propensities toward religious thinking. Froude's attitude, like that of scientists in general, of course was that the human race has progressed largely through overcoming such natural propensities, through attacking primitive impulses and submitting them to the control of reason. Experience taught Froude that natural promptings, inferences from insufficient data, conclusions based on desires, were

[15] June 27, 1847.

more often untrue than true, at least so far as a standard of truth could be established through scientific verification. Truth was to Froude immutable, and he felt that supernatural truths, in so far as they could be examined at all, ought to be susceptible of corroboration by the natural means of science.[16] Religious and scientific truth should, he believed, fit into a single system wherein neither contradicted the other. The methods of investigation might differ in the two cases, he admitted, but he could not conceive of ultimate contradiction.

In relying on human experience, as he did very wisely, Newman unfortunately neglected another fact of experience quite as universally recognized as instinctive promptings; namely, that the certainty which these promptings often produce is frequently proved ephemeral. Where we have been once certain, we come later to be uncertain, and the unsettlement generally arises from an accretion of new information. Froude knew for himself how impossible it was to hold a single tenet as indefectibly certain; even a remote possibility of new information weighing against his conclusion was nevertheless sufficient for him to keep his mind "settled in unsettlement." Newman had gracefully overleaped this difficulty by making a scholastic distinction between convictions and certitudes. He admitted that one might be positive about a particular

---

[16] This was also the orthodox view. It will be noted that of the two men it was not Newman but William Froude who was on the side of orthodoxy, for theologians all maintained, as Newman acknowledged, that the truths of religion were to be proved by the logical reasoning processes of the *Verstand*. Newman did not argue that his own method was the only means for proving religious truth, but he maintained that it was the actual method of the generality of men, who were naturally unversed in technical theology, and that the method was a valid one.

point and yet at a later date for reasons perhaps of additional information change one's mind. In such a case one had not attained a state of certitude; one had attained only a conviction. In a state of conviction one allowed, if only subconsciously, for the possibility of a change of opinion. Certitude was a right conviction which one *knew* was right, and it was indefectible. Froude of course had only convictions. He could not attain a state of unchanging certitude because such confidence in the durability of human opinion was impossible to him as it was to many another.

Direct and specific sources for Newman's thought were remarkably few. Newman's greatest indebtedness seems to have been to the Zeitgeist—to what he called in the *Apologia* a " spirit afloat "; for there was undoubtedly something in the very air which affected like minds in similar fashion at the same time. The Catholic revivals in France and Germany closely paralleled the Oxford Movement, and all three owed much of their motivating force to the prevailing spirit of Romanticism. It was partly at least the Zeitgeist which led the Abbé Bautain, one of the French Traditionalists, to develop an argument for religious belief almost identical with the thought of Newman's *University Sermons*. Like Newman he relied on insight, on a super-reasoning faculty of the mind, for arriving at belief. Though Newman was aware of the French movement, he owed nothing to it, and denied specifically any indebtedness to the *fidéism* of Bautain, as he likewise denied conscious indebtedness to Coleridge. Newman's thought was an extraordinarily personal product, but one of the definite influences upon him, which can be established with certainty, was that of William Froude, and it is to an account of that influence that the following pages are devoted.

II

CORRESPONDENCE THROUGH 1845

II

CORRESPONDENCE THROUGH 1845

UNTIL after the appearance of Tract 90 in 1841, Newman was so busily engaged upon the work of the Movement that he had little time for serious correspondence with any but his immediate circle. When he was finally repudiated by his Bishop and the Heads of Houses, he knew that his place in the Movement was lost forever. Removed thus suddenly from the storm center, he had more time for reflection, and immediately there came a new flood of doubts and questions, engulfing him in a mental anguish almost without parallel. It was only when his personal anxiety became nearly unbearable that he sought outside friends for solace, and among those to whom he turned most readily were the Froudes.

During the years when the Tracts were appearing, Froude was absorbed in his engineering projects, and without the occasion of pressing necessity his correspondence with Newman was naturally upon matters of little more than passing importance. His work took him about considerably, however, and he frequently stopped with Newman at Oxford. The conversations that passed between them came to mean more and more to Newman as the months went by, and this was largely due to the fact that Newman recognized the young Froude as already a man of penetrating intellect and of great promise in the field of science. Outside testimony to Froude's mounting reputation had reached his ears, and he was pleased on one occasion to pass on to Mrs. Froude the remark of a friend that all England was full of Froude's praise. "His particular word was," he wrote, "that he was so very 'conscientious.' I am pretty sure I have heard other stories to the same effect." [1]

It was thus naturally out of trivialities that Newman's correspondence developed slowly into a means whereby he could relieve the pent emotions of his solitary communing. He had also known Mrs. Froude while she was still Miss Holdsworth, and shortly after her marriage he had even proposed to enlist her aid in the Oxford Movement. He learned by chance, in 1839, that she cherished not unusual maidenly aspirations for literary fame and that she had actually completed a novel highly religious in tone. A zealous friend showed him the manuscript, which he thought had some real merit, so he suggested that she set about in a serious way to write children's stories which should have a pointed religious moral. Her courage fell short, however, and she did not attempt to contribute to the fictional propaganda [2] of the Movement as Newman encouraged her to do in his letter:

> As to your declining the undertaking which I was bold enough to suggest through Miss Froude, I can say nothing more of course; but still I have a right to my private opinion, and do maintain it, that you could, I feel sure, be of use to the cause of Catholic Truth in the way I mentioned. . . . though I am far from saying that there is no other way in which you will be of as much or more. Certainly we do want tales on our side very much—to take people's imagination—as such works as Geraldine on the one side and Father Clement on the other show—and I should rejoice if such persons as yourself gave the composition of them a fair trial.[3]

---

[1] August 3, 1843.
[2] For an account of the deliberate propaganda in the form of fiction, see Joseph Ellis Baker, *The Novel and the Oxford Movement* (Princeton University Press, 1932).
[3] April 27, 1838.

WILLIAM FROUDE

Newman's correspondence with Froude before 1843 was of a similarly light tone. Sometimes he wrote rather involved answers to the polite questions Froude put to him, and on one occasion at least he ended with a touch of self-conscious humor, "Am I not writing stuff?" But as his path became daily more obscured, the temper of his letters changed. Romanism grew into an all absorbing thought. In 1840 he wrote Mrs. Froude:

> If it comes in your way, you would be interested by a little book of Miss Agnew's called the Young Communicants. Were you inclined to Romanism, I would not mention it to you. It should not be dipped into, but read through.[4]

This problem became more and more pressing as the correspondence continued and Newman was depending more and more upon the Froudes for sympathetic discussion. A paragraph to Mrs. Froude shows something of his state of mind in 1843 and of the increasing reliance he was placing upon his former pupil:

> It quite put me out, when William was here, to think how little I could explain myself to him. In truth, it is hardly possible to do so in a little while. Everything I said seemed to be shot out like bullets, round and hard and sudden. Arguments ought to grow out of the mind, but when you see friends but seldom, there is a necessary abuse of a certain medium of communication which is the very life of conversation or discussion. I could only lament it; *and wish, what at present seems out of the question, that we were thrown together more.*[5]

How dark for Newman was this year 1843, every reader of the *Apologia* knows. He was moving steadily though with the utmost deliberation toward Rome. Few dared offer him spiritual comfort, and few besides Mrs. Froude even dared inquire into the state of his

[4] November 8, 1840.   [5] December 9, 1843. Italics mine.

mind. His friends could but stand by in suspense, expecting the development which they all believed to be imminent.

At the same time Froude was also experiencing the gravest religious difficulties which were, however, leading him in a quite opposite direction. To his scientific mind the fundamental basis of religious belief seemed unstable. He expressed his doubts to Newman, and it was in attempting to explain away some difficulties of Froude's that Newman began, on April 2, 1844, the series of long letters which follow. He had not proceeded far when he began to entertain fears lest his explanation increase rather than alleviate Froude's perplexities, but so great was Newman's personal relief in recording his intimate history that he continued to write not for Froude's benefit but for the entirely personal satisfaction of thinking through to a conclusion his own problem. These letters give an intimate picture of Newman's mind as it was during the time of severest strain. Years later, in 1859, he recalled these letters and, as he said proudly, " copied them all in a single day " to preserve so exact a record of his thoughts. In writing the *Apologia* he used a few paragraphs from them as the best explanation of the state of his mind.

He addressed the first letter to Froude, but fearing that he might be from home, he directed the remaining ones to Mrs. Froude, since it was well understood that the correspondence was a three-sided one.

April 2, 1844

And now, my dear W. on a subject which I have long wished to write to you about—and thought myself quite cruel towards you and your wife not to do so—but it is so very great a trouble to me to write about it, that after putting it off again and again, now that I have begun, I feel as if I had nothing to say and that I had better not have taken up my pen. My matter and all spirit has gone out of me, and I am already thoroughly disgusted. Not the least part of my disgust is having mentioned to you and her anything on the subject, [the] disgusting thought comes across me, what if after all I have unsettled and harassed you both for nothing? Not that I ever (alas) am myself settling down into an acquiescence in things as they are, but a fearful feeling visits me, and almost tempts me, as if I *must* go forward, *lest* I shall have made a great fuss about nothing, and wantonly disturbed you. It seems as if I now could not possibly relapse into that happy state of contentment with things as they are, without a bitter remorse rising as to my conduct towards you. At the same time I repeat I must say in truth my reason is more and more averse to the existing state of things.

I think at times, if I could have summoned resolution, I had something to say on a remark you made about your own chief perplexity, but I am quite disgusted with myself now, and am quite languid and unequal (through disgust) to any exertion. It does seem unpardonable in a person like myself, who sit at home and speculate, to be thrusting his doubts upon sincere and single minded persons, like you and your wife. I can only say, I feel it to be odious. But now being in that odius position, the question is whether I shall not relieve your mind, My dear W. by speaking more than by a now unreasonable silence.

And now having got as far as this, and really not wishing for any answer (which will only disgust me more with myself, for I know how kind it will be), I shall take the rest of one post, and wait till tomorrow before inflicting anything more upon you.

Ever yr and yr wife's affectionate friend,

J. H. N.

Littlemore.
April 3/44.

My dear Mrs. Froude,

Pray take my writing as a proof of my anxiety to act rightly towards persons I love so much as William and you—and please continue to do what I am sure you do already, remember at sacred times and places me and my difficulties.

What I was going to remark upon yesterday was what seemed W's chief distress, viz. that my changing my opinion seemed to unsettle one's confidence in truth and falsehood as external things, and led one to be as suspicious of the new opinion as one became distrustful of the old. Now in what I shall say, I am not going to speak in favour of my second thoughts in comparison of my first, but against such scepticism and unsettlement about truth and falsehood generally—the idea of which is very painful—at least this will be my main subject.[6]

The case with me then was this, and not surely an unnatural one:—as a matter of feeling and of duty I threw myself into the system which I found myself in. I saw that the English Church had a theological idea or theory as such, as I took it up. I read Laud on Tradition, and thought it (as I still think it) very masterly. The Anglican theory was very distinctive. I admired it, and took it on faith. It did not (I think) occur to me to doubt it, and I saw that it was *able*, and supported by learning, and I felt it was a *duty* to maintain it. Further on looking into antiquity and reading the Fathers, I saw such portions of it as I examined fully confirmed (e. g. the Supremacy of Scripture). There was only one question about which I had a doubt, viz. whether it would *work*, for it had never been more than a paper system.

Of course it is a difficulty to speak from memory of feelings and thoughts which belong to eight and nine years ago, and

---

[6] This paragraph and the following one were incorporated, with slight changes, into the *Apologia*. See Newman's *Apologia Pro Vita Sua, The Two Versions of 1864 & 1865,* ed. Wilfrid Ward (Lond. 1913), pp. 297-98.

moreover to an exciting and busy time—yet I trust I have represented my former self correctly, though such a representation needs as much caution as I can give it.

One thing of course I saw clearly—that there was a great risk of Anglican principles running into Roman. They i. e., primitive, had done so once—as I notice in the Advertisements to my third volume of Sermons—they might do so again. And I felt both admiration and love of Rome, as far as I dare. This is plain from one of the notes in smaller type on the Translation of Vincentino in Records of the Church (in the Tracts) No. xxiv, in which I say, "Considering the high gifts and the strong claims of the Church of Rome, etc. on our admiration, reverence, love, and gratitude, how could we withstand it, as we do; how could we refrain from being melted into tenderness and rushing into communion with it, but for the words of Truth itself etc. 'He that loveth father or mother more than Me etc.?'" [7] Other of the early Tracts show the same thing—and some of the Lyras " O Mother Church of Rome " and " O that thy creed were sound."

Nothing then but a strong positive difficulty or repulsion has kept me from surrendering my heart to the authority of the Church of Rome; a repulsive principle, not growing out of Catholic, Anglican or Primitive doctrine, in the way in which I viewed that doctrine, but something antagonistic, arising from *particular doctrines* of the Church of Rome, particular historical views, etc., etc.

And this very circumstance led me to be violent against the church of Rome—because it was the only way of resisting it. A bulwark and breakwater was necessary to the position of the English Church and theory. And in being violent, I was not acting on private judgment against so great a Communion, but I had the authority, or rather the command of all our Divines, who, doubtless from the same constraining necessity, have ever been violent against her also. To be violent against Rome was to be dutiful to England, as well as a measure of necessity for the English theory.

[7] *Records of the Church*, No. xxiv, " The Holy Church Throughout All the World Doth Acknowledge Thee," p. 7.

Now on all these respects I was contrasted, as you may easily see, with Hurrell Froude. He went by no theory, he was bent on defending no system, he was no Advocate, laughed at economies, merely investigated—and in consequence, and just in the same proportion, did not attack the Church of Rome, and disliked attacks upon it.

But to be brief—such were my feelings and views from 1833 to 1839. It was my great aim to build up the English system into something like consistency, to develop its idea, to get rid of anomalies, and to harmonize precedents and documents. I thought, and still think, its theory a great one. What then was my dismay or excitement, call you which you will, when in 1839 it flashed upon me in the course of reading the Fathers, which I had hitherto read with the eyes of our own Divines, that (not only was it a theory never realized) but a theory unproved or rather disproved by Antiquity? but I must stop.

> Your affecte friend
> John H. Newman.

> Littlemore.
> April 4/44.
> In bonâ Domini—(all good gifts to you at this season).

My dear Mrs. Froude,

Without waiting for any answer from you, here I go on, making up pretty considerably for my delay and silence; and all about myself.

So far from my change of opinion having any fair tendency to unsettle persons as to truth and falsehood as objective realities, it should be considered whether such change is not necessary should truth be a real objective thing, and made to confront a person who has been brought up in a system *short of* truth. Surely the *continuance* of a person who wishes to go right in a wrong system, and not his giving it up, would be that which militated against the objectiveness of Truth—leading to the suspicion that one thing and another were equally pleasing to our Maker where men were sincere.[8]

Nor surely is it a thing that I need be sorry for that I defended the system in which I found myself, and have had to unsay my words. For is it not one's duty, instead of beginning with criticism, to throw oneself generously into that form of religion which is providentially put before one? Is it right, is it not wrong, to begin with private judgment? May we not on the other hand look for a blessing *through* obedience even to an erroneous system, and a guidance by means of it out of it? Were those who were strict and conscientious in their Judaism, or those who were lukewarm and sceptical, more likely to be led into Christianity when Christ came? Yet in proportion to their previous zeal, would be their appearance of inconsistency. Certainly I have always contended that obedience even to an erring conscience was the way to gain light—and that it mattered not when a man began, so that he began on what came to hand and in faith—that anything might become a divine method of Truth, that to the pure all things are pure, and have a self-correcting virtue and a power of germinating. And though I have no right at all to assume that this mercy is granted to me, yet the fact that a person in my situation *may* have it granted seems to me to remove the perplexity which my change of opinion may occasion.

I am writing in a most miserably prosy way, which I cannot just now get out of. Perhaps it will go of itself presently. Well, but it may be said, I have said it to myself [9]—"Why however did you *publish?* had you waited quietly, you would have changed your opinion without any of the misery, which now is involved in the change, of disappointing and distressing people." I answer that things are so bound up together as to form a whole, and one cannot tell what is not a condition of what. I do not see how possibly I could have

---

[8] This and the following paragraph appear in the *Apologia*, ed. Ward, pp. 298-99.

[9] The four following sentences (ending at the asterisk) are in the *Apologia*, ed. Ward, p. 299.

published the Tracts or other works professing to defend our Church without accompanying them with a strong protest or argument against Rome. The one obvious objection against the whole Anglican line is, that it is Roman, and I really think there is no alternative between silence altogether and forming a theory and attacking the Roman system.* In my lectures on the Prophetical Office I apologise for doing the latter from " the circumstances of the moment," both because " till they (persons who attack the " Holy Cath. Church ") do more *than they have hitherto done,*" " they hazard a deviation into Romanism etc " and next because in teaching that doctrine " the plan of attacking Romanism " is " the most convenient way of showing what our own views are ". As far as I recollect I give the same *defensive* reason in the first of the " Tracts agst Romanism," No. 71 I think. Either then I was obliged to commit myself to a theory of the Church and against Rome publicly and argumentatively, or not a Tract could be written. And where I myself should now be in opinion as well as many others, if no Tracts had appeared, is a speculation quite beyond me.

Nothing indeed all through this course of things strikes me as more strange than the intertwining of things good and bad. E. g. one is tempted to say, knowing what misery has resulted and does result from Dr Hawkins being Provost of Oriel, " O that Hurrell's wish had been accomplished of placing Keble in his place! " But if Keble had been Provost, I for one should probably be Tutor of Oriel to this day. What great things K. might have done then, of course, is quite hid from us—they would have been great—but we should have never been dismissed from the Tuition, we (K., R. H. F., and I.) should never have turned our minds so keenly to other subjects, not a Tract would have been written. I should have gone on with Mathematics (which I was bent on doing and did, till Jenkyns *on the ground* of my leaving the Tutorship, introduced me to *Rose* and so to the History of Arianism) I should have gone on with Niebuhr and Aristotle.

You must not suppose I am arguing against my having

committed all sorts of faults in my *mode* of doing things, so much so, that all the comfort I might have had is taken away, of feeling an *assurance* that I have been brought on by a divine guidance to my present point. Alas! though I do not think there is anything in the mere fact of my change to show that I am wrong or to unsettle people, yet I have so bad a conscience in details as to have *very little* claim to feel confidence that I am right. This of course is what keeps me back. And now this unsufferable prose has exhausted my paper. O, my dear Mrs Froude, I am very must disgusted at it.

Ever yrs affectionately,
John H. Newman.

Littlemore.
Good Friday Evening.
April 5, 1844.

My dear Mrs Froude,[10]

I write with some apprehension lest I should be making a great fuss about nothing and to no good—and yet I think too that what I have said and shall say may tend to make you less uncomfortable.

My confidence against the Church of Rome lay in two things, first my feeling that we had the Apostolical Succession—next my conviction that her peculiar doctrines were not held by the Fathers.

As to the first of these, I acknowledged great irregularity in the transmission, and vast and various disorders and faults in our Church. But I got over all by the parallel of the Jewish Church, which was a Church when Christ came, in spite of anomalies as great as ours. My view is drawn out in my last Lecture on the Prophetical Office.

As to the second it was to me as clear as day (as it is now)

---

[10] Brief excerpts from this letter and the following are given in *Correspondence of John Henry Newman with John Keble and others, 1839-1845* (London, 1917), pp. 24-26.

that the honors paid in the Church of Rome to St Mary were not primitive. On this I rested our case mainly for those honors are at once the furthest removed from primitive usage and especially characteristic of the Roman Church. I have drawn out the general argument in Lecture ii on " Romanism as neglectful of Antiquity."

My defence of the English Church against Rome was conducted under the shelter of these two convictions, with the expression of which my lectures begin and end. They were written in 1834-1837; and during 1836 and 7 the Tracts against Rome.

In the Summer of 1839 I was led in the course of my *regular reading* (which is a point on which some stress might be laid) to the Monophysite controversy, and to the Council of Chalcedon and St Leo's works inclusively. I found what surprised me very much. It struck me at once, but when it began to assume an unsettling character I do not recollect—but I found more matter for serious thought in that history than in anything I had read. The Council of Ch. is the fourth A. D. 452 Ecumenical Council, which it is generally considered the English Church receives. Our Divines consider its opponents heretics, as denying that " Jesus Christ has come in the flesh ". Eutyches was condemned then, he said there was but one nature in our Lord. Now I cannot bring together all the strange things I found in its history. I found the Eastern Church under the superintendence (as I may call it) of Pope Leo. I found that *he* had made the Fathers of the Council unsay their decree and pass another, so that (humanly speaking) we owe it to Pope Leo at this day that the Catholic Church holds the true doctrine. I found that Pope Leo based his authority upon St Peter. I found the Fathers of the Council crying out " Peter hath spoken by the mouth of Leo ", when they altered their decree. I found a portentously large body of Christians thrown into schism by this Council, at this day the Churches of Egypt, Syria (in part) and Armenia; and the schismatics not like the Arians, of a rationalist, but with a theology of a warm and elevating character. I found that they appealed, and with much plausibility, to certain of the Fathers, as St Athanasius and St Cyril of Alex.—that they professed to be maintainers of the antiquity—that they called their opponents (the Catholics) *Chalcedonians,* as we call the R. C.'s Tridentines, that their cause was taken up by the civil power, and created a contention between Emperors and the Church. Further I found there was a large middle party as well as an extreme. There was a distinct Via Media, which indeed the Emperor took up, and there was a large body who went on for some centuries without Bishops. I am writing from memory, but I am sure I am right in all points of consequence—and in a word I found a complete and wonderful parallel, as if a prophecy, of the state of the Reformation controversy, and that we were on the Anti-Catholic side.

I will go on with this part of the subject at the expense of the order of time. I add then that from that time to this, the view thus brought before me has grown upon me. I had hitherto read ecclesiastical history with the eyes of our Divines, and taken what they said on faith, but now I had got *a key,* which interpreted large passages of history which had been locked up from me. I found everywhere one and the same picture, prophetic of our present state, the Church in communion with Rome decreeing, and heretics resisting. Especially as regards the Arian controversy, how could I be so blind before! except that I looked at things bit by bit, instead of putting them together. There was Pope Julius resisting the whole East in defence of St Athanasius, the Eusebians at the great Council of Antioch resisting him, and he appealing to his own authority (in which the historians support him) and declaring that he filled the See of St Peter. The lapse of Pope Liberius, carefully as it needs considering, does not interfere with the general view. There were two parties, a Via Media, and an extreme, both heretical, but the Via Media containing pious men, whom St. Athanasius and others sympathise in—there were the kings of the earth taking up the heresy against the Church — there was precisely the same appeal to Scripture, which now attains, and that grounded on a literal interpretation of its text, to which St Athanasius always opposes the "ecclesiastical sense"—there was the same complaint of introducing novel and unscriptural terms into the Creed of the Church, "Consubstantial", and "Transubstantiation" being both of philosophical origin, and if Trent has opposed some previous Councils (which I do not recollect) at least the Nicene Council adopted the very term "Consubstantial" which a celebrated Council of Antioch 60 or 70 years before condemned or discountenanced.

When shall I come to an end?

Ever yrs affectionately,
John H. Newman.

Littlemore.
Easter Tuesday.
April 9/44.

My dear Mrs Froude,

I have received your kind letter this morning and at present cannot make up my mind whether I ought to send you any more of these harassing letters. Not that I meant them either to be many or harassing, I set about overcoming what seemed to be a difficulty pressing on William—and I suspect I both exaggerated it, and have been led into a great error in my way of meeting it. However I write on, whether you see it or not, writing (since I have begun to do, what I had no notice of doing in my first letter to you) to complete what otherwise probably I may never get myself to do.

What I described in my last was the view that burst upon me, that separation from the body of Christendom, and again, or especially, from the see of Rome, is (to those who would go by primitive views of Christianity) a *presumption* of error. I cannot recollect by what degrees or at what time it became an unsettling principle in my mind, though I perfectly recollect the lively feelings produced in me by the Monophysite history. These I mentioned to H. Wilberforce among others at the end of July when we met at the consecration of the New Church at Otterbourne. But I cannot make out that I realised them practically till the end of the Long Vacation, then something else occurred to give them very serious force.

I know how very coolly, that is, historically, I must seem to you to be writing on these most serious matters. But it does no good to be roundabout. If I am to write, I must write plainly, yet I can hardly get myself to say what now comes, though it is difficult to say why. At the end of the Long Vac. (1839) a number of the Dublin Review appeared containing an Article by Dr Wiseman which made some talk in Oxford. I looked at it, and treated it very lightly. Persons who (I suppose) half took up our views, said we were bound to answer it, meaning it was a great difficulty in the way of the Anglican theory. I recollect saying it was "all the old story" and would not think about it. I do not know what made me take up the Number again, but I found it on careful attention to contain so powerful an argument that I became (I may say) excited about it. I was leaving Oxford for a few weeks, in the course of which I paid visits to Rogers and to H. Wilberforce, and to both I mentioned that I was shaken in my confidence in the Anglican theory, but to no one else.

The argument in the Article in question was drawn from the History of the Donatists, and was directed to show that the English Church was in schism. The fact to which the Monophysite controversy had opened my eyes, that antagonists of Rome, and churches in isolation, were always wrong in primitive times, and which I had felt as a presumption against ourselves, this article went on to maintain as a recognized principle and rule in those same ages. It professed that the *fact* of isolation and opposition was *always taken* as a *sufficient* condemnation of bodies so circumstanced, and to that extent, that the question was not asked how *that the quarrel arose?* which was right, and which wrong? who made the separation? but that the *fact* of separation was reckoned anciently as decisive against the body separated. This was argued chiefly from the language of St Augustine as elicited in the Donatist controversy, and the same sort of *minute* parallel was drawn between the state of the Donatists and our own, which I had felt on reading the history of the Monophysites.

On my return to Oxford, my immediate business was to set about answering this argument. It is my sincere belief and principle that it is right to resist doubts and to put aside objections to the form of doctrine and the religious system in which we find ourselves. I think such resistance pleasing to God. If it is His will to lead us from them, if the doubt comes from Him, He will repeat the suggestion, He will call us again as He called Samuel, He will make our way clear to us. Fancies, excitement, feelings go and never return—truth comes again and is importunate. The system in which we have been placed is God's voice to us till He supersede it, and those means by which He supersedes it must be more distinct than the impression produced on us by that system itself. Accordingly I then set about, as I have since, to keep myself in my own place. What I wrote appeared as an article in the British Critic in January (I think) 1840, under the title of "Catholicity of the English Church",[11] and, though important practical effects followed from the shock I had received, the view of the subject which it contains kept me quiet for nearly two years, that is, till the autumn of 1841.

The practical effects which I speak of, were such as these:— 1. to attempt to give up St. Mary's. I brought this before the College in 1840, wishing to retain Littlemore, but the Provost would not hear of the separation of the Living. In 1841 I took the Cottages I now inhabit, and from the beginning of 1841 I had a curate at St. Mary's and gradually took less and less share in the duty there. Last year, as you know, I resigned it. 2. I gave up society etc., in Oxford as far as might be. The affair of No. 90 was an excuse for this. In consequence, i. e. in 1841, our theological meetings at Pusey's came to an end, and my weekly evening parties also. 3. I gave up the British Critic in the spring of 1841, this was

[11] Pp. 40-88.

settled, before the affair of No. 90. 4. As far as possible, I left off writing on any subjects of the Day (except in Sermons, then I felt it my duty while I held St Mary's). My contributions to the Tracts, as a course, came to an end in 1838. In 1840 I added the Devotions of Bp Andrewes—and nothing else, except indeed No. 90, which shall be mentioned presently. As to my University Sermons I went on with them as finishing a course; the last, which has made some talk, I wrote quite lately, but I will speak of this elsewhere, if I ever write so much. Except No. 90, I have not as far as I remember written anything on subjects of the Day since 1838, six years. I have already excepted Sermons. (I suppose you will say certain letters in the Times in the beginning of 1841 are exceptions. I was *pressed* to write them.) 5. Of course I became very careful of saying things against Rome. In new Editions of my volumes I corrected many passages, and at the end of 1842, I took measures for the publication of a retractation of certain passages which called for it. I published an article on anti-Christ in the B. C. in 1840 I think. (By the bye several B. C. articles form another important exception since 1838.) 6. I was very desirous of an adjustment, or at least of the contemplation of an adjustment between ourselves and the Church of Rome, and without feeling I knew enough about the matter to dare to pronounce that it might be upon the basis of the Council of Trent, I hoped it might be so. And feeling very strongly the corruptions in the Church, I felt more and more inclined to regard them, as had very frequently been done, by our writers, as *in* the Church, not *of* the Church. 7. No. 90 originated in various causes. The desire just mentioned of drawing towards Rome; a feeling of the need which various persons had to know *how* Catholicly to interpret certain articles; a feeling as if our opponents had a right to ask and ought to be told, and as if it were disingenuous, and would clearly seem so, not to state plainly how we reconciled our subscriptions with out opinions; and moreover a hope that to *state* the Catholic interpretation was to *make* it; for what was allowed, became de facto an interpretation. I did not foresee the great opposition made to it and such condemnation from authority. I had taken up my notes here for writing it in Lent 1840, but I did not write it till the beginning of 1841.

At the time of publication of No. 90, I was 1. desirous of union with Rome, i. e. Church with Church. 2. I was strongly opposed to the idea of *individual* moves. 3. I thought the *practical* system of Rome very corrupt and thought those corruptions *balanced* our quasi-schism (I have drawn out my view in the B. C. of July 1841, Article on Private Judgment). 4. I thought my own occupation quite gone in the Anglican Church. My feeling is shown in a Preface I wrote to Nelson's Life of Bull (I think) in 1840.

You will clearly see, if you see this letter at all, that it is written with a minuteness consistent with what I have stated in the first lines of it, rather than in a way which will interest you.

Yours affectionate Friend,
John H. Newman.

Littlemore,
April 12/44.

My dear Mrs Froude,

I am in great perplexity to know what to do about proceeding with my letters. I began with a view of relieving a difficulty of Wm's, not of urging arguments ags^t our existing position. But in my last letter I was betrayed into doing so. All I can say is that it was natural, since in your letter written before you received it, you ask for some of the considerations which had weighed with me.

Now I think before asking me to proceed, you and Wm would seriously think whether it is *good* for you that I should do so. You alone can answer this question. I don't see why leaving off where I do should leave you in suspense. That you must be quite as much if I told you all I have to tell. The great remedy of all uneasiness is to feel that we are in God's hands, and to entertain an earnest desire to do His will. Surely while you are in doubt, and much more when you are not in doubt, and only know of others being in doubt, your duty is to go on quietly in faith, not thinking of the future. And if we know what our *duty* is, what else need we care about not knowing?

Be sure that I am in no danger of moving at present. Of course I cannot prophesy what may happen towards me from without; but I can have no intention of doing anything, or I should not just now have put out those Sermons. . .

Ever yrs aff^{ly}
John H. Newman.

Littlemore.
May 19, 1844.

My dear Mrs Froude,

I said in my last that difficulties presented themselves to me in the Anglican theory of the Church from which the Roman is free. On both theories the Church is considered, as the Creed declares it, *one*—now the meaning of "one" is simple, if "one Church" means one *kingdom,* one body politic, but in what sense do Anglicans consider it one? They consider it a *succession,* propagated through different countries, independent in each country and claiming the adherence of Christians in this or that country to itself as it exists in this or that country. Each bishop is isolated from every other and supreme in his own diocese, and if he unites with others, it is only as the civil power or his own choice happens to unite him. He claims obedience yet without claiming to be a depository and transmitter of true *doctrine,* the succession being a point of order, not a condition and witness of Christian faith. And all other bishops or religious bodies acting in his diocese without his leave are schismatical. Now if this be so, the question occurs in what sense do Anglicans consider the Church *one?* in what sense are Rome and England one?

If Rome and England *are* one, what is meant by the common phrase of "the church of our baptism"? Baptism is "one", and admits into the "one body"; not into any local society. A child baptized by a clergyman of Oxford is not admitted into that diocese or Church, but into the Catholic Body, which is diffused throughout the world, and which is the real Church "of his baptism". It puzzled me to make out, in what sense, on the hypothesis that Rome and England formed one Church, a man changed his Church who went from the English to the Roman branch, any more than he changed it, if he communicated here with the Church of Oxford, there with the Church of London. He changed his *faith* indeed; that is another matter; but how was he guilty of schism, how could he *change* his Church, when there was no *other* Church to change to?

To meet this difficulty Anglicans are forced into the following argument—that is, I believe so; and certainly I was, and have expressed it, among other places, in the Article on the Catholicity of the English Church and in a note at p. 150 of the Oxford Translation of St Cyprian's Treatises. (No—I have explained the *general theory* in these places). They say, that since there is but one Bishop and Church in each place, and our succession, not the Roman, has possession in England, therefore the Roman succession and Church are intruders here. But surely this is very technical and unreal; for who can deny that the true difference between us and Rome is one of *doctrine and practice*? Yet such an explanation sinks that difference altogether, and reduces our quarrel with Rome to one of ecclesiastical arrangement. Its irrelevance is shown as soon as you put the question of members of our Church going abroad; are they to communicate with the Roman Church in places where that Church has possession? If we are one Church with Rome, only locally distinct, they ought, yet few would feel it right to do so; and if they do not, we are *not* one Church with Rome. The Anglican theory then cannot be acted upon, it is a mere set of words—facts confute it.

It was, I think, in the beginning of 1840, that a lawyer,

with whom I was slightly acquainted wrote me several letters on this subject, in opposition to Palmer, which had the effect of convincing me that it was absurd to call the Roman Catholics schismatics in England. As I recollect, his plain argument was, how preposterous that a man who across the Channel believes in purgatory, the Mass, the Pope's Supremacy etc. must all of a sudden, if he comes to England, change his creed and worship, and become member of a local community which denies all he has hitherto received? This led me to investigate the Anglican theory of local Episcopacy itself, from which these absurdities follow, and I found it as untenable as its consequences; as a few words will show.

May 29. I think it is Hooker who tells us the distinction between "Bishops by restraint" and "Bishops at large". Bishops by restraint are Bishops with a certain definite jurisdiction. Bishops at large are Bishops over the *whole* Church. Now I believe it is generally granted that this "restraint" is the consequence of a byelaw of the Church, and that local jurisdiction, which it implies, is not of the essence of the Episcopate. In the theory of Episcopacy there is never more than *one* Bishop in the whole Church—for every Bishop is but the shadow and repetition of every other. Every Bishop has the full Episcopate in his own person, as in a firm every partner has all the responsibilities of the whole house. They are, to use a law phrase, "joint tenants" in power, or (as St Cyprian expresses it) they have the Episcopate "in solidum". There is then one and one only Bishop in the Church, with a universal jurisdiction, the Vicar of Christ, and the Pastor of Souls. *Each* Bishop is *all this* in *his essential* character; such is the theory which I think you will find in Bingham, and among ancient writers in St Cyprian's Treatise De Unitate. . . . But now it is obvious how inconvenient, or rather how impossible such a theory is in practice, while men are men. If a thousand absolute and independent monarchs rule over the whole heritage of Christ, what is to secure their agreement? who is to decide their differences? This being so, by a series of bye laws and usages (similar to that by which three Bishops at least are necessary for a consecration, though in the theory and really, one is enough) the intrinsic power of individual Bishops is curtailed, and one is put under another. The great majority of Bishops deprive themselves of their intrinsic universal jurisdiction and take a subordinate place under others, and all limit their *immediate* jurisdiction to some particular spot, or what is called a Diocese. They are then called what they all are in fact, " Bishops by restraint ", and thence results the great Patriarchal system. They divide between them, for the sake of order, their own power—one is a suffragan, another a metropolitan, another a private. And again, since such an arrangement depends on byelaws or canons, when matters arise of greater consequence than canons, e. g. matters of faith, then all parties return to first principles and rights. Thus, as you will read in Bingham, during the Arian troubles each Catholic Bishop considered himself quite free to consecrate and order things anywhere, when Arianism prevailed. They then became Bishops at large again, or had a universal jurisdiction.

But if this be so, how absurd is it, I was going to say hypocritical, when we have actually broken from Rome in matters of faith and order, when we have asserted an independence which can only be defended by an abolition of all usages in canons, then again to effect a delicacy and profess an etiquette on the point of local jurisdiction. This is straining out a gnat and swallowing a camel. We have a greater right to place a Bishop at Malta, than we had to disobey the Pope, local episcopacy and the Popedom—stand on the same basis, viz. that of canons. And the R. Cs have as great a right to create a Church in England, or we to create a Church out of the Roman communion—if their congregations are disobedient to the Bishop of London or Winchester, yet so are the Dioceses of London and Winchester to the Pope. At the Reformation the Patriarchal system was broken up as in Arian times, Bishops at large succeeded to Bishops by restraint, and though we may have rules among ourselves, as Roman Catholics have, yet England and Rome, viewed as Churches, each claims its inherent original jurisdiction over the whole Church. If at the Reformation there was division indeed, but not a schism, much less are the particular acts growing out of that division deserving that serious name. The presence of Rome in England and of England in Rome is the legitimate and necessary consequence of that great event.

Moreover, this being the case, we see how preposterous it is to talk of the Pope's "usurped power". As to his exercising power over the *whole Church,* he only does what all Bishops have a right to do, except they are restrained by definite provisions. As to his claiming power over the Bishops, he only does it by usage, by prescription, by the canons as the Archbishop of Canterbury. If he goes beyond these warrants he acts unjustifiably. While he can appeal to them, he is blameless. What he possesses, is either what he retains or what he has received. And in saying this, I am not going to the question whether his power is by divine right or not, even though it has been brought about by natural and human means, it may be a fulfilment of the prophetic promise to St Peter as recorded in xvi of St Matthew.

A further conclusion seemed to follow from what has been said. If the ecumenical authority of the Pope has been created, not by his exaltation but by the canonical depression of other Bishops, and is no assumption, but the result of a voluntary arrangement, it follows that while it is lawful as being in their own power, it must necessarily be gradual as being the consequence of their positive acts. Canons are not framed, nor do usages obtain, in a day—nor do the dispositions and ordinances which are the subject of them. The Papacy then could not but be of slow growth, and if it were the subject of prophecy in Matt. xvi, there is still greater reason for saying so. All then that we look for in antiquity, is tendencies and beginnings of its greatness, and these are found abundantly. This is the further conclusion which I meant, and with reference to it I will bring this long letter to an end.

I write from memory, and therefore may make some mistakes in detail, though I am correct on the whole. St Clement, Bishop of Rome, (vid. Library of Fathers, vol. 8, p. 44, note f) who is mentioned by St Paul, wrote a pastoral letter which is extant to the Church of Corinth. St Ignatius addresses the Church of Rome as the Church " which presides " or " is the first see in the country of the Romans ". Dionysius of Corinth in the second century speaks of its alms and benevolences as extending all over the Church. St Irenaeus in the same century calls it the Church with which all others must concur. Pope Victor at the same time threatened the Churches of Asia Minor with excommunication. Tertullian, Origen and St Cyprian use language in the third like Irenaeus's. Pope Stephen repeats towards St Cyprian the threat of Pope Victor. Pope Dionysius is appealed to against Dionysius Bp of Alexandria in a matter of doctrine by Alexandrians, entertains the appeal, requires an explanation of him, and receives it and the Roman civil government submits the deprivation of Paul, Bp of Antioch, to the decision of the see of Rome. In the fourth century St Athanasius and his friends appeal to the Roman see, and St Jerome professes in a matter of doctrine and in the choice of a patriarch of Antioch, to rule himself by its decision. Moreover in every case the view whether of doctrine or discipline taken by the see of Rome, ultimately prevailed, and, if success is the token of truth, is the true one. It is the Pope who has determined the rule for observing Easter, and for treating the baptisms of heretics, who has confirmed or pronounced the condemnation of Arianism, Apollinarianism, Pelagianism, and the other numerous heresies which distracted the early Church. He appears to exercise an infallibility which in after ages he has more distinctly claimed.

All these things being considered, I was forced to admit that the doctrine of the Papacy was a primitive one—for

1st. If we do not allow of developments, especially in a matter which from the nature of the case *requires* time for its due exhibition, hardly any doctrine can be proved by antiquity.

2. Nor is it anything to the purpose that the Pope's power was withstood in early times, e. g. by St Cyprian—for when a doctrine or ordinance has to be developed, collision or disturbances seem previous conditions of its final adjustment.

3. Nor is it to the purpose that certain passages such as those which I have referred to above from writers of the first centuries may otherwise be explained—for the question is

which of the two interpretations is the more likely—and the event seems to suggest the true interpretation, as in the case of a prophecy.

But I am getting hard and dry, if I have not been so all along.

Ever yr affectionate friend,
John H. Newman.

P. S. Your letter of this morning has led to my finishing this. Since my object in writing has ceased to be that with which I began (viz. that of removing a painful feeling which William seemed to have) I have become both somewhat indolent about writing, and also very anxious about the *effect* of my letters to you. Both these feelings will account for my long silence. The same change of purpose makes me indifferent as to hearing what you think about my letters, so that I am made certain they do not unsettle you, for I am not writing with a purpose so much as finishing a subject I may not otherwise get myself to work out.

May 28/44.

My dear Mrs Froude,

I have got a letter to you half written—but I cannot get over the feeling that I may be unsettling you, and doing something cowardly, this has kept me from finishing and sending it, when I took it up again. I wish I knew precisely what state you are in, and what I might safely say to you and what not. Your last letter quite satisfied me—but I do not know that I have a right to judge now from what you wrote six weeks ago.

By the bye as I am writing, I will say this much to you about my own matters—that I do not mind it being said, as an historical fact, whenever you care to do so and have opportunity, that you have reason and know that I was very much unsettled on the subject of Rome in the year 1839. I should not like you to say anything about my *present* state of mind, nor as to *how* you got your information. Perhaps these two conditions will prevent your saying anything—but my feeling is, that it is unfair that people who think well of me should not be made acquainted with this *fact,* considering so much has come of it. I know it will shock them, but it is better than a greater shock afterwards and it is very unpleasant to be trusted when I do not deserve it. How are W's eyes.

> Ever yrs,
> John H. Newman.

> Littlemore.
> July 14, 1844.

My dear Mrs Froude,

I find the subject I have now got into is endless, and I must cut it short. I meant to have drawn out the mode in which I have got reconciled to the (apparently) modern portions of the Roman system. It has been by applying to them that *principle* which, as my last letter showed, had long been in my mind, the principle of developments. From the time I wrote the Arians, or at least from 1836, I have had in my thoughts, though I could not bring it out, that argument or theory, which at last appeared as my closing University Sermon.[12] It was delayed as long as I could in the series of Sermons from inability, or fear of not doing justice to it, as it ought, in the due order, to have preceded the one before it.

Yet I must confess that the Sermon does not, as Palmer has observed in his Pamphlet, go the whole length of theory which is necessary for the Roman system, and that something is still necessary to the discussion of the *theory,* though I have no difficulties about receiving the system in matter of fact. The kind of considerations which do weigh with me, are such as the following:—[13]

1. I am far more certain (according to the Fathers) that

---

[12] Sermon XV, "The Theory of Developments in Religious Doctrine."

[13] Newman used the following statements in the *Apologia,* ed. Ward, p. 290.

we *are* in a state of culpable separation *than* that developments do *not* exist under the gospel, and that the Roman developments are *not* true ones.

2. I am far more certain that *our* (modern) doctrines are wrong, *than* that the Roman (modern) doctrines are wrong.

3. Granting that the Roman (special) doctrines are not found drawn out in the early Church, yet I think there is sufficient trace of them in it, to recommend and prove them, *on the hypothesis* of the Church having a divine guidance, though not sufficient to prove them by itself. So that the question simply turns on the nature of the promise of the Spirit made to the Church.

4. The proof of the *Roman* (special) doctrines is as strong (or stronger) in Antiquity, as that of certain doctrines which *both we and the Romans* hold. E. g. there is more evidence in Antiquity for the necessity of Unity than for that of the Apostolical succession—for the supremacy of the see of Rome than for the Presence in the Eucharist—for the practice of Invocation than for certain books in the present Canon of Scripture, etc., etc.

5. The analogy of the Old Testament and the New leads to the acknowledgement of doctrinal developments. E. g. the prophetical notices concerning our Lord before His coming. Again the gradual revelation of the calling of the Gentiles through St Peter and St Paul. Again, the distinct theological announcements of St John's gospel compared with those which preceded it. Again it is undeniable that the doctrine of the Holy Trinity, as we now hold it, is historically the result of a great deal of discipline and controversy, of much heresy and much antagonist development. Again the rule for baptizing heretics, or of infant baptism etc., etc. was unsettled and contested in early times, but at last universally obtained as it is at present.

And now I have said enough on the whole subject—and I cannot get over the feeling that I have intruded it upon you.

Your affectionate friend,
John H. Newman.

These letters give a point of view somewhat different from that of the *Apologia*. When writing to the Froudes Newman was simply giving the arguments which weighed with him in renouncing the Anglican Church, whereas in the *Apologia* he was disclosing his intellectual history primarily to disprove the charge of lying laid against him by Kingsley, and consequently he elaborated even the smallest points in his effort to show a sincerity of purpose. His private letters proceeded along more strictly intellectual lines, and it is evident that when he wrote them he was entirely convinced on purely rational grounds that he could not remain an Anglican. And yet in spite of intellectual certainty, he did not find it immediately possible to make a final decision of such moment, and had he done so it would have been against the fundamental principle of his thinking. It was not until his "whole being" had been convinced of the correctness of his step that he was able to move. Not until that multitude of small reasons in themselves insignificant had finally a cumulative force equal to certainty could Newman make confession of faith in the Catholic Church.

Newman waited until his illative sense permitted him to move with certitude. The illative sense is in part dependent upon emotion, and it is indubitable that Newman's decision in some degree was made from feelings of sympathy for the Roman Communion. The forces at work in him were confusing. He says in his letters to the Froudes that " nothing but a strong positive difficulty kept me from surrendering my heart to the Church of Rome," and in writing to them he confined his remarks largely to an account of the " paper logic " by which alone he wished to reach his decision, slighting the emotional causes which had influenced him. It is the portrayal of these subtle emotional causes at work within him that gives to the *Apologia* a poignancy and an appeal to be found in no other autobiography.

So far as simple rationalization goes, nearly the whole story is in these few letters. There are, however, certain omissions and differences of emphasis to be noted in the letters. Since these were necessarily short in comparison with his formal work, Newman either did not wish or intend to analyze philosophically " the concatenation of argument by which the mind ascends from its first to its final idea," [14] and this broader question of philosophy, which he touched on more fully in the *Apologia*, is of no small importance, particularly in view of his later writings. The letters do not suggest that Newman was considering seriously the effect of his conversion upon the larger issue, the cause of Liberalism, a question to which he does give attention in the *Apologia*. Nor does one feel, after reading the letters, that, in 1844, Newman considered Mariolatry really " the essence of Rome's offence." The affair of the Jerusalem Bishopric, which in the *Apologia* is listed as a ' final blow,' is entirely passed over in the letters, and one may suspect that it outraged Newman's sense of decorum rather more than it actually offended against any laws of ecclesiastical polity.

As to the all-important Tract 90, the attitude seems to be the same in the letters as in the *Apologia*, although the letters do imply that the *experimentum crucis* was made for much more personal reasons than those offered in the *Apologia*, where Newman says that the motivation for publishing the Tract was

the restlessness, actual and perspective, of those who neither

---

[14] *Apologia*, p. 291.

liked the *Via Media,* nor any strong judgment against Rome. I had been enjoined, I think by my Bishop, to keep these men straight, and I wished so to do: but their tangible difficulty was subscription to the Articles; and thus the question of the Articles came before me. It was thrown in our teeth; "How can you manage to sign the Articles? they are directly against Rome" "Against Rome?" I made answer, "What do you mean by 'Rome?'" and then I proceeded to make distinctions. . . .[15]

The final Tract was written, it would seem more likely, in an effort to "think things through," and he apparently hoped to benefit by such criticism as it might receive to help him toward a solution of the problem. The unexpected uproar, however, actually deprived him of his place in the Movement, and from that time on his progress to Rome was accelerated.

Partly to acknowledge the great debt he owed to their affectionate regard, so different from the accustomed treatment he describes below, Newman kept both William Froude and his wife informed of his melancholy situation. He wrote to Mrs. Froude:

> Littlemore.
> Nov. 12, 1844.
>
> My dear Mrs Froude,
>
> Lest you and William should be fidgetted, I write a line to say that I have no reason to suppose that any thing is happening to me now, or will for I do not know how long.
>
> The pain I suffer from the thought of the distress I am causing cannot be described, and of the loss of kind opinion on the part of those I desire to be well with. The unsettling so many peaceable, innocent minds is a most overpowering thought, and at this moment my heart literally aches and has for some days. I am conscious of no motive but that of obey-

[15] *Apologia,* p. 176.

ing an urgent imperative call of duty—alas what am I not sacrificing and if after all it is for a dream?

Please do not grudge that I should thus write to you. I had not meant, when I began, to do more than dissipate any immediate alarm you might be under. But let me, as I am writing, ask you to think of me at sacred times, as I daresay you do. My spirits have not yet given away. But what with this long continued inward secret trial, and the unwearied violence of the attacks upon me, most cruel, though they mean it not so, at a time when I most need peace, I am just now in straits. Dying people are commonly left in quiet. If I *am*, as people think, unsettled, what great thoughtlessness to be watching every look and gesture and reporting it at the market place!

This does not call for any answer, as you will see.

> Believe me, My dear Mrs Froude.
> Your and Wm's affectionate friend
> John H. Newman.

Prophetic of the situation which was before long to arise in the Froude family itself is Newman's letter to Mrs. Froude less than a year before his conversion.

> Littlemore,
> Dec. 8/44.

My dear Mrs Froude,

I only write to thank you for your kind letter, since business hindered William from conveying to you any news of me. It is kind in you to speak as you do, but the trouble I am introducing into families, as well as into individual minds, does and must from time to time afflict me most severely. Take the case of a person losing all confidence in his present creed, because he finds he must go further or go back yet unable to go further. Or the case of a mind actually lapsing into a sort of infidelity, because he finds the same arguments which are available for Christianity are available for Rome. Or think of a husband and wife divided, not able to pray together, and totally perplexed to know how they possibly are to educate their children. Or one sister dying, and another unable to sooth her anxieties or to receive the last Communion with her. There are the things which weigh so heavily upon me.

Meanwhile, this, I suppose, is worth noting. I have always said, O that I may be guided by something external to my own mind. Now the series of measures which are in progress against Ward, do seem likely to constitute such a direction. If he is expelled the University for holding certain things which I hold (however I may dissent from other of his views, or dissent from the propriety of putting those certain things forward) I do not see how I can remain a member of it either. And if the Bishops virtually, if not formally, acquiesce in such a sentence, and the majority or bulk of the Clergy and Laity either by silence or by avowed approbation, what is left but to believe that such views, and the persons who hold them, are repudiated by the Church? The series of measures in prospect is quite independent of any act of mine, and an external coincidence with my own personal convictions.

It surprised me much to see that article about me in the English Churchman some weeks ago. So far is plain now, that things are not secret which hitherto you have kept secret, and you may use your own discretion about them, as far as I am concerned.

Yrs very affectionately,
John H. Newman.

The struggle was nearly over in the Spring of 1845; Newman was waiting only to complete his *Development of Christian Doctrine*, which is the "something" he refers to in the following letter as intending to publish before Christmas.

Littlemore.
April 20/45.

My dear Mrs Froude,[16]

I have long been thinking of writing to you, both as wishing it, and as thinking you might be anxious.

It is a melancholy thing to report progress—melancholy, that is, to the hearers. Were it not for the pain I am giving, I seem to myself to be likely to have no pain. I do not know, but so it seems to me, as if I had no doubt or difficulty. My mind certainly is in a very different state from what it was this time last year. It is so made up.

I do not name a longer time than next Christmas before a change—but of course I cannot anticipate the course of things, which may accidently retard or accelerate it. I am getting more callous about consequences, from feeling that there are dangers on all sides, on any course of conduct; so my mind is like the nautical needle in a box cased all round with iron.

As far as I can anticipate, I shall do as follows:—give up my fellowship in October or November, and publish something between that time and Christmas . . .

With love to W. and the little children especially my dear R. H. F.

Ever yours very sincerely,
John H. Newman.

P. S. Every kind remembrance to the Archdeacon.

In spite of the pressure of work which almost entirely absorbed him, Newman continued to send short notes full of those affectionate touches which in spite of external demands upon him never ceased to characterize his correspondence. He was much affected by the interest, not entirely sympathetic, with which Archdeacon Froude was watching his progress.

[16] Portions of this and the following letter appear in *Correspondence of John Henry Newman with John Keble and others, 1839-45*, pp. 377-379.

Littlemore.
June 1, 1845.

My dear Mrs Froude,

Your very kind letter was most welcome, and I had intended long before this to have told you so. But I am very busy, and with a sort of work which tires my body as much as my mind.

Did I tell you I was preparing a book of some sort to advertise people how things stood with me? I think I am bound to do this, if I can—but you may so suppose how difficult a thing it is to do. And I have for some time been overworked. When I had finished the translation and notes of St Athanasius, at the end of last year, I said I would give myself six months rest—for really I require it. And then I found all of a sudden this new work come before me, and I could not deny its claim on me. I have been thinking about some work or other since last March year, and turning the subject in my mind at odd times—yet in spite of that, I have lost, if that is the word when it could not be helped, or rather consumed several months this Spring, in working upon it in ways which will not turn to any direct account. I have had to remodel my plan, and what it will be at last I cannot yet foretell. All I know is that body and mind are getting wearied together, and the book not yet written through for the first time.

This then is my occupation at present, with many interruptions, which hardly serve as reliefs. It will be a sort of obscure philosophical work, if I manage to do it, with little to interest and much to disappoint. But I hate making a splash; and of course I hate unsettling people, if I *could* do so; I would rather write something which wd sink into their minds.

I am very anxious about the Archdeacon, and interested in what you say of him. But the trial is all over now—at least I hope so. I hope everywhere the shock is getting over, as you say it is generally in your neighbourhood.

I am not telling anyone that I am writing; else people will be expecting something which they will not have. These late confident reports frightened me—for if the whole world believes I am going, I suppose I ought for the appearance of the thing to resign my Fellowship at once: whereas I do not wish to do so before October, because that is the time I have fixed.

Thank you for what you say about my own comparative composure at present. Certainly I am not, except at times, in the state of distress I was in last Autumn. My mind is a great deal more made up.

Ever yours very sincerely,
John H. Newman.

P. S. On reading this over, I see it is all about myself. I have been reading your own letter over again. How very kind it is! what a contrast.

Froude visited Newman only a few days before his conversion, which in this case was not to mark a parting of friends. Of what passed between them on that occasion there is no record, but something of Newman's personal distress may be seen from the last paragraph of his note:

Littlemore.
Sept. 26/45.

My dear William,

I shall be here at any time next week, so far as I know and I need not say how glad I shall be to see you. But knowing your engagements, I shall not expect you till I see you. And so I say of little Hurrell it would rejoice me indeed to set eyes upon him, but this is not a time of year for a child to travel. It is very kind in you thinking of it.

The illness (so to call it) you heard of, was last winter. I was pulled down for months and have not got over it now, I dread this winter. But there is nothing to show for it, so to say. I am as usual outwardly—and I shd be very unthankful if I did not add that I am quite sure (if it is right to say so) that I am not *really* unwell, only pulled down.

Ever yrs aff^{ly}
J. H. N.

Newman joined the Catholic Church on the evening of October 8, 1845. From a leading figure in the Establishment he was to become a Roman priest, generally overshadowed and sometimes deliberately obscured. He renounced the worldly position and the preferment that might readily have been his in the Anglican Church, and turned deliberately to a faith unpopular and even despised. His motive was intellectual honesty, for he had a conviction amounting to certitude that in the Roman belief alone lay the truth, and it was to the discovery of truth that Newman had ever devoted himself. After his conversion he no longer had any doubts; his mind was at peace. But though there were no doubts, there remained difficulties, and the chief of these was to explain in any logical fashion *how* one might believe in the Catholic Church. To the question of the reasonable means of arriving at belief Newman gave the best thought of his later life, and his answer to that question is his philosophical masterpiece. During all the years that he occupied himself in reflecting on this problem, amid a multitude of other severe and often harassing labors, Newman continued to correspond with the Froudes and to enjoy short visits from William at the Oratory. In these years he submitted to Froude certain philosophical ideas for criticism, secure in the knowledge that however at variance with his own might be the scientific opinions of his friend, never would the criticism he sought give him such pain as at times he had had to suffer at the rude hands, among others, of the Anglican bishops. Their correspondence did not cease until William Froude's death.

III

CORRESPONDENCE THROUGH MARCH, 1857

III

CORRESPONDENCE THROUGH MARCH, 1857

NEWMAN'S conversion to Rome, intellectually, was complete. Never did he remotely consider a return to the Anglican faith in which he had left so many of his dearest friends. But to Oxford itself, and particularly to Oriel, he never ceased to look longingly, and it was the greatest tragedy of his life that he was never allowed to return to the scenes of his triumphs, there again to gather to his voice a band of followers who would echo, now in the true church, the old cry, *Credo in Newmannum*. Without friends in Rome, he was sent not to Oxford but to Ireland, where every door was shut in his face. Instead of leading a movement of thought, he was set to teaching little boys Latin plays—from expurgated editions. Shorn of all position and influence, the greatest English mind in the Roman church was left to occupy itself with the *quotidiana solicitudo* of little things. "They have put me on the shelf," he wrote, "but they cannot prevent me from peeping out." And no indignity he was made to suffer shook even for a moment his faith in the church. Mere unpleasantness of a temporal nature was as nothing compared to the gift of spiritual grace which he had gained. He had entered into a new world to share in a divine dispensation, and he submitted in all humility and obedience to whatever vexations might also be his share. He wished most devoutly to bring others to a state of spiritual peace which should equal his own. To those friends from whom he was not entirely cut off after 1845, he wrote of his great satisfaction in the

Roman faith, and to some few of these his letters were even of a proselytizing sort.

In continuing his correspondence with the Froudes Newman dwelt almost entirely on religious topics now more than ever close to his heart. His mind, no longer unsettled, spoke out more positively. Self-examination gave way to explanation and description of this new happiness. Arguments, historical and epistemological, flooded upon him and were poured out in conversation and in letters. Among those to whom he talked most positively and freely was, of course, William Froude. But Froude had, by 1845, so far progressed toward an habitual state of scepticism that Newman's assertions ceased to gain credence as once they had. Too many arguments of an opposite nature presented themselves to Froude. He had long realized the futility of seeking absolute certitude, and he could not readily accept as genuine Newman's Catholic convictions when he had seen him so recently convinced of quite different tenets. Newman felt that his change was a final step from the false, or at least the half false, to the absolute truth; he admitted no possibility of further change. Froude on the other hand felt that one change of opinion increased, or certainly did not decrease, the chances of additional changes. This was, and for some time had been, an issue between them. The first note of argument was introduced into their correspondence when Froude wrote a long and carefully reasoned letter which he sent to Rome where Newman had gone, but by some mischance it never reached its destination. Froude took Newman's consequent failure to reply to mean that he either could not or cared not to answer the arguments set down in it, and for more than two years the correspondence ceased. In the Spring of 1847, however, Froude ventured again to intrude his arguments upon Newman, who at once replied, apologizing for his long silence.

The correspondence as it was resumed was devoted almost entirely to an exposition of Catholic claims. Newman addressed his letters largely to Mrs. Froude, since he felt her bias was naturally toward Rome, but he was scrupulous never to urge his position too strongly lest he bring upon her mind an unsettlement as dreadful as his own had once been. Realizing the danger as well as the impossibility of attempting to bring about any sudden conversion, he wrote with a view to pointing out ways of advancing, leaving her to draw for herself the conclusions. Two letters show the delicacy with which he put forth his points.

Mary Vale, Perry Bar: June 16, 1848.

My dear Mrs Froude,[1]

I answer your kind and touching letter just received immediately. How could you suppose I do not feel the warmest attachment and the most affectionate thoughts towards you and yours?

And now first about myself, since you are kindly anxious about me. It is my handwriting that distresses you; but it has been so for years. I seem to have sprained some muscles. I can't put my finger on the place—but I never write without some pain. And it does not seem that there is any help.

As to health, I never was better or so well. The only indisposition is that I am always tired, but that I think is merely owing to the growth of years. As time goes on too, one's features grow more heavy. At least I feel it an effort to brighten up. Or rather, I believe those long years of anxiety have stamped themselves on my face—and now that they are

[1] Wilfred Ward, *The Life of John Henry Cardinal Newman* (London, 1912), I, 239-41.

at an end, yet I cannot change what has become a physical effect.

And now you know all about me, as far as I am able, or can get myself, to talk of myself. I will but add that the Hand of God is most wonderfully on me, that I am full of blessing and privilege, that I never have had even the temptation for an instant to feel a misgiving about the great step I took in 1845, that the hollowness of High Churchism (or whatever it is called) is to me so very clear that it surprises me, (not that persons should not see it at once) but that any should not see it at last, and, also, I must add that I do not think it safe for any one who does see it, not to action his conviction of it *at once*.

Oh—that I were near you, and could have a talk with you—but then I should need great grace to know what to say to you. This is one thing that keeps me silent, it is, dear friend, because I don't know what to say to you. If I had more faith, I should doubtless know well enough; I should then say, " Come to the Church, and *you will find all you seek*." I *have myself* found all I seek. " I have all and abound "—my every want has been supplied, and as it has in all persons, whom I know at all well, who have become Catholics,—but still the fidget comes on me, " What if they fail? What if they go back? What if they find their faith tried? What if they relax into a lukewarm state? What if they do not fall into prudent and good hands?" It is strange I should say so, when I have instances of the comfort and peace of those very persons for whom I feared on their conversions.

But I will tell you what I think on the whole, though you do not ask me, in two sentences; 1. that it is the duty of those who feel themselves called towards the Church to obey it; 2. that they must *expect* trial, when in it, and think it only so much gain when they have it not. This last indeed is nothing more than the spirit moving, " when thou come to serve the Lord, prepare thy soul for temptation."

I would not bring anyone into the Church on the ground which you put as against the Church of England, viz: that all hopes are failing. Not that I do not value, not that I do not now feel, the *stimulus* which comes from bright prospects, but that one ought not to come, if it can be helped, on such inferior grounds. Now this world is a world of trouble. You must come to the Church, not to avoid it, but to save your soul. If this is the motive, all is right. You cannot be disappointed, but the other motive is dangerous.

I was thinking of you this morning, when I said Mass. Oh that you were safe in the True Fold. I think you will be one day. You will then have the blessedness of seeing God face to face. You will have the blessedness of finding, when you enter a Church, a Treasure Unutterable, the Presence of the Eternal Word Incarnate, the Wisdom of the Father who, even when He had done His work, would not leave us, but rejoices still to humble Himself by abiding in places on earth, for our sakes, while He reigns not the less on the right hand of God. To know too that you are in the Communion of Saints, to know that you have cast your lot among all those Blessed Servants of God who are the choice fruit of His Passion, that you have their intercessions on high, that you may address them, and above all the Glorious Mother of God, what thoughts can be greater than these? And to feel yourself surrounded by all holy arms and defences, with the Sacraments week by week, with the Priests' Benedictions, with crucifixes and rosaries which have been blessed, with holy water, with places or with acts to which Indulgences have been attached, and the " whole Armour of God "—and to know that, when you die, you will not be forgotten, that you will be sent out of the world with the holy unctions upon you, and will be followed with masses and prayers; to know in short that the Atonement of Christ is not a thing at a distance, or like the sun standing ever against us and separated off from us, but that we are surrounded by an atmosphere and are in a medium, through which His warmth and light flow in upon us on every side, what can one ask, what can one desire, more than this?

Yet I do not disguise that Catholicism is a *different religion* from Anglicanism. You must come to learn that religion which the Apostles introduced and which was in the world long before the Reformation was dreamed of, but a religion not so easy and natural to you, or congenial, because you have been bred up in another from your youth.

Excuse all this, as you will, my dear Mrs. Froude, and excuse the rambling character of this whole letter, and believe me,

> Ever yours most affectionately,
>
> John H. Newman.

P. S. I should rejoice to see William at any time; but I am going to London soon.

> Mary Vale, Perry Bar: June 27, 1848.

My dear Mrs. Froude,[2]

One of the thoughts which most painfully weighed on my mind, when I began to see that I must be a Catholic, if not the most painful of all, was that I was unsettling many, who, having been without definite faith till I and others made them what is called Anglo-Catholics, were likely, on my confessing that to be a delusion which I had taught them was a reality, instead of passing on with me to a second creed, to relapse into scepticism . . .

But oh, my dear Mrs. Froude, what an awful state is that of doubt, if permitted, if acquiesced in, if habitual; considering that faith, implicit faith, is the fundamental grace of the Gospel, and condition of its benefits? The very notion of doubt is then only endurable, when a person is firmly resolved to embrace the Truth, whatever it be, at whatever cost, when once it is brought home to him, and immediately;—praying the while that he may, as soon as possible, be brought to the knowledge of it. If you, my most dear Sister or Daughter, as you chose to let me call you, really can say in your heart, that you will submit to the Truth, though you cannot prove it,

[2] Ward, *Life*, I, 242.

directly your reason tells you where it lies, I am comforted about you; but do search your conscience on this point. Are you quite sure you respond, as you should, to God's grace leading you on? Are you sure that you do not take "obedience," (to allude to the Sermon you speak of) instead of faith, when you should only take it as the way to faith? resting in it, instead of using it . . .

I wish you would consider whether you have a right notion how to gain faith. It is, we know, the Gift of God, but I am speaking of it as a human process and attained by human means. Faith then is not a conclusion from premises, but the result of an act of the *will*, following upon a *conviction* that to believe is a *duty*. The simple question you have to ask yourself is, " Have I a *conviction* that I *ought* to accept the (Roman) Catholic Faith as God's word? " if not, at least, " do I *tend* to such a conviction? " or " am I *near* upon it "? For directly you have a conviction that you ought to believe, reason has done its part, and what is wanted for faith is, not proof, but *will* . . . . We are answerable for what we choose to believe; if we believe lightly, or if we are hard of belief, in either case we do wrong. With love to William,

Ever yours affectionately,
J. H. Newman.

This last letter is of considerable importance in the history of Newman's relations with the Froudes. In it he gives one of his clearest definitions of faith [3] as " not a conclusion from premises, but the result of an act of the *will*, following upon a conviction that to believe is a *duty*." Such a definition marks the gulf separating him from any scientific thinker like Froude and is likewise a measure of the tenuity of his whole argument for faith. According to Newman an apprecia-

---

[3] Reprinted in Erich Przywara's summary of Newman's thought, *A Newman Synthesis* (London, 1932), pp. 118-19.

tion of the evidence for revelation will lead logically to the conclusion that one must believe what revelation teaches. After assuming that God exists and that He has given evidences of His existence, Newman imposes it as a *duty* unreservedly to accept these evidences of God's existence. Faced with this duty to believe, the good Christian must exercise his will to make himself do so. In this manner of arriving at belief the intellectual process in so far as it employs the reason, the *Verstand*, is reduced to a minimum, and the very important principle that belief should be proportionate to the evidence is abjured, and a contrary principle set up, namely, that one must believe even though the evidence be, on strictly rational grounds, inadequate. Even a vague comprehension of the implications of revelation is deemed sufficient ground for attaining logically a firm belief. One might in the freedom of one's will withhold assent, but such an act would be undutiful.

An argument which so completely ignored the laws of evidence and the possibility of error could but be repulsive to William Froude, and it became another point of divergence. Froude could not allow, nor could other scientists, that there was any duty to believe anything, unless, indeed, it was proved by the most rigorous of tests. " Our ' will ' ", Froude wrote on another occasion, " has no function in reference to the formation or maintenance of our ' Belief,' but that of insisting that all probalities on either side shall be honestly regarded, and weighed, and borne in mind." [4]

The point illustrates the different attitudes of the two men toward truth. To Froude the truth was something external to the mind but discernible if sought diligently,

---

[4] December 29, 1859.

honestly, and in the proper manner, that is, by a judicial and entirely unprejudiced weighing of evidence. And the evidence for arriving at true conclusions was, he maintained, equally open to all men to see and to evaluate. Newman held entirely different principles. The cardinal point in his philosophy was that a special disposition of mind was indispensable to the discovery of special truths; to discover religious truth one had to be religiously minded. The evidence was not, he believed, open alike to all men, and the reason why an irreligious man could not perceive religious truth was that, in the first place, much of the evidence for religion was hidden from him; he had not the proper intellectual equipment to discover it.

Newman's argument was particularly difficult to controvert from the very fact that he would not allow that his opponents had the means of seeing and knowing some things which were perfectly plain to himself. Froude in his later letters pointed out this fallacy, as it seemed to him, in Newman's argument, and asked repeatedly for an explanation of *how* the religious man saw so easily things hidden from other equally sincere but unfortunately irreligious men. It was partly an attempt to explain the psychological process peculiar to religious minds that led Newman to develop his theory of the illative sense.

For six years Newman continued to write to both the Froudes, though more particularly to Mrs. Froude, letters like the above. Throughout the correspondence he unfailingly exhibited what was one of the chief characteristics of his personality, a faculty for entering into the minds of those about him. It was this extraordinary ability that made him so keenly appreciate the mental struggles of his friends and made him hesitate to argue too forcibly. Typical of his whole manner is the humility with which he reassures Mrs. Froude after she had written him of the difficulties which seemed to make it impossible for her as yet to acknowledge the Catholic faith.

Mary Vale,
Perry Bar.
July 3, 1848.

My dear Mrs Froude,

Do not suppose your letter disappointed me, or pained me, except as I was indeed pained to see how much pain it had given you to write it, as when you talk of fearing that we are parted for ever. And beside this, you actually confess to so much pain, that so far I too am very much pained, but not at all of anything you have said about your state of mind.

You do not do me justice, if you think I did not know and enter into that state of mind, before I read your letter. Nor am I now going to argue with you. Far from it, God's teaching is more powerful than man's; and to you and William more suitable. To Him I leave you securely and cheerfully. May He be over you, and William and your children, and bring you forward in His own way! Do what you so religiously propose to do. I mean, cultivate that great virtue, faith, which I acknowledge may be possessed in the Anglican Church; which, knowing your earnestness and sincerity, I will believe that you possess in it, if you tell me so.

This is not inconsistent with my holding that in *reality* there is " no medium between scepticism and Catholicism," and on the contrary it is quite consistent with my saying that, if you join us, it must be " to save your soul ": sentiments, which I am surprised you are startled at, seeing I have invariably expressed them, e. g. in the Essay on Development, in Loss and Gain, in all my private letters written three years since, to Dr Pusey (in spite of his published letter about me, which for that reason pained, as misrepresenting, me) and, I cannot but think, at that time, or before, to you.

But to return. Your postscript suggests one remark. It seems you are going to "make yourself believe again" as in 1834: but recollect, though you can believe what you choose, you must believe what you ought. Now, assuming *duty* proved, still you cannot believe without 1. a *creed.* 2. an *authority* which will not mislead you. At least put these first *before you,* even if (as you imply) you do not think in your position you need *prove* them. E. g. the Catholic makes his act of faith 1. in the *Creed,* and the so called Creed of Pope Pius, and the other dogmatic teaching of the Roman Church—2. in the *authority* of the Roman Church. This at least is intelligible. You too should have your answers, if you are to bring your good intention to a right issue;—and, if I may add one remark, which I suppose you will allow, you should either have in your hand your whole Creed, or be able to ascertain any point of it, when necessary.

I have done. May all blessings be with you all. I shall remember you daily in the Mass.

Ever aff^{ly} yours,
John H. Newman.

Oratory,
Birmingham.
July 14, 1849.

My dear Mrs Froude,

This is the 16th anniversary of the commencement of the Oxford movement, St Bonaventura's day. I had long been made very anxious about you and W^m, whether I would or not—and at length the day tempts me to write to you.

Were I convinced that you had an honest thorough persuasion that the Established Church was the Catholic Apostolic Church, I should grieve, but sh^d have a certain satisfaction. But knowing some traits of your state of mind before the Oxford movement began, I cannot keep from anxiety, and you will pardon me (I am sure) for it, but you sh^d be relapsing into it. Anthony Froude's sad book [5] seems to come as an

---

[5] *The Nemesis of Faith* (Chapman, 1849).

external tempter to unbelieving views—while the feebleness, helplessness, of the Anglican system seems unlikely to exert any influence over you as its antagonist.

My fears may certainly be groundless—but O what an awful thing it is, should you be in the way of losing your faith. If God has for many years been forming a habit of faith in you, and at length He put before you the true object of that faith, and you have refused to accept it, and so have lost a state of mind which cannot live except in its object! Alas, how many instances do we see around us of a wrecked and ruined faith! of those who either deliberately, or at least virtually, have preferred scepticism to Rome! Surely faith is the gift of God, as it was in St Paul's day, and the divine election is as wonderful now as then.

No—the sons of God are born, not of the will of man, but of God. What passionate efforts have I witnessed after the conversion of individuals: What multitudes of masses were said for Pusey. I have heard those who said that they *would* have him. I have never liked this way of talking, and have never given into it. I believe that it is an awful thing to say Mass for a conversion, for it may bring down a judgment on the person whom you say it for, if it does not convert him. I have fancied I have seen this. No, the election is with God; we can but cooperate with Him and we must submit to His decision.

> "Too happy, if, that dreadful day,
> Thy life be given thee as a prey."

Yet it is dreadful to have to give up the hopes of those one has loved so much, and has worked with.

No—men will not believe one testimony, and they must at length learn its truth when it is too late to believe. We can only say "Whereas we were blind, now we see"—they answer "that is what any Methodist fanatic may say." Well then, do you take us for Methodist fanatics? do you take me for a hot headed dreamer? have you the face to say so? Yes— you have. When you can't get out of the difficulty otherwise, you hint that I am mad. I have seen in a newspaper, published at the time of my conversion, the fact, not argued, but announced in a long article, apparently by a clergyman, stated that it was well known to my friends. O shame, how will this plea stand at the last day, nothing is sacred, private feelings are not sacred, when a way to Rome is laid open. Close that way, though with the bodies of your friends, yes, to the letter —for others said to me "I had rather see you die than join the Church of Rome."

Four years are nearly passed since that time. How do matters stand now? What additional evidence has the Established system? It is a system which cannot hold anyone who thinks —it is a Church which cannot detain anyone who acts upon his thought. Thinkers go one way or the other. Now I may be mistaken all this time, and you may be satisfied with it— yet I cannot believe it.

But if not, O my dear Mrs Froude, are you content to live and die without *faith*?

Ever yours affect^{ly}
John H. Newman.

While letters of this sort were passing between Mrs. Froude and Newman, William Froude was actively opposing the arguments in conversations with both his wife and Newman. His position remained throughout that one ought never to employ the will to reach a conclusion. The only fair method was to wait patiently for evidence to pile up sufficient to make for absolute certainty. Frequent change made each new position more dubious rather than more conclusive. Consequently he did not move forward even by slow steps but preferred to assemble all the evidence and, on the basis of probabilities derived from it, to make a single and, if necessary, considerable change of opinion. Unswayed by the defection of a few individuals to the Catholic Church, he waited to see whether large numbers of rationally minded men would also go over. For him this waiting was but a manner of gathering the evidence; the more men of proved intellectual capabilities who went over, the greater the probability in favor of their side. But few men of consequence made any immediate move toward Rome, and this strengthened Froude's conviction that Newman was acting alone.

Froude's argument on this point, which he wrote to Newman in April, 1847, has not been preserved, nor is Newman's reply among the collection of papers now in the possession of the Froude family. Four years later, however, in writing to an unidentified correspondent, possibly Mrs. Ward, Newman made rather detailed reference to Froude's earlier criticisms, which may be inferred from Newman's remarks. The letter as given below differs in several small but important points from Wilfrid Ward's reading (*Life,* I, 622-24), which in one instance (paragraph two) completely reverses Froude's statement.[6]

As to dear W. F.'s letter of April / 47 it contains two arguments against inquiry in religious matters, and [for] acquiescence in doubt.

He speaks of a state of mind " certainly different from a long and anxious condition of change "—one in which one is " taking *no steps* for oneself or apparently getting nearer to a change." And he thinks there is " an intelligible reason for following it."

One of his two grounds is, that, whereas I once said " that, if I am right in my doubts, what had happened to me might *happen to others* also," "*till then* the least unsatisfactory course seems to be to stand still." He refers particularly to Keble and Pusey. He says too that perhaps " some happy re-union may be yet in store."

---

[6] The letter was written in 1851, and not, as Ward states (I, 622), in 1850.

Now as to Keble and Pusey, perhaps it is more wonderful that a person of my age (when I left them) should have embraced a new religion, than that they should not have done the same. But valeant quantum; I will not touch the argument, as derived from them, here. Yet my anticipation, as W. F. has recorded it, has been remarkably fulfilled. One after another, moving not as a party, but one by one, unwillingly, because they could not help it, men of mature age, from 40 to past 50, in all professions and states, numbers have done what I have done since the date of W. F.'s letter;—such as Manning, R. Wilberforce, H. Wilberforce, Allies, Dodsworth, Hope Scott, Badeley, Bellasis, Bowyer, Monsell, Sir John Simeon, Dr Duke, Biddalph Phillipps, Dean Madavori, Bp Ives, the de Veres, H. Bowden, Mrs Bowden, Lady Lothian, Lady G. Fullerton, Lord H. Kerr, etc. I cannot help thinking it was dangerous for W. F. to have recourse to this argument. It is surely much easier to account for Keble and Pusey not moving, Catholicism being true than for all these new persons moving, Catholicism being not true. And, whereas it was the fashion at first to use this argument, as W. F. does in 1847, *against* us—I think it ought to have its weight now for us. It was the fashion then to say " O, Newman is by himself. We don't deny his weight—but no one else of any name has gone —and are we to go by one man? " Times are altered now.

Alas! this was not W. F's real reason, this, which solvitur ambulando. I did not get his letter at Rome. I had not the opportunity of answering it; but, so far, Time has answered it for me in a way which solves all doubt, by bringing Truth, his glorious daughter, out. The second ground is his real reason, which Time will solve too—tho' not so soon—alas! that he will not anticipate its unsoundness, as he has not anticipated the unsoundness of the former.

The second argument which W. F. uses with himself is that he has got less and less to see his way in any such questions, and that there is least private judgment in making no judgment at all.

This means, when brought out, this:—that, without denying there is a truth, which would be absurd (for either Catholicism, as we hold it, is from God or it is not) we have not been vouchsafed means sufficient for getting at the truth: and therefore if we attempt it, it is like attempting to fly, or to sail on the Atlantic in a pleasure boat without compass—we shall be lost—or we shall go wrong—or we shall be ever at sea—or, if we attain anything better than what we start from, it will be by accident.

I do not undervalue at all the speciousness of this argument. But I would remark at once, that almost all truth "lies in a well."

Does not this saying imply two things 1. that it is hard to find, yet 2. that it may be found?

If it is so in other subject matters, may it not be so in religion too?

Is it not likely to be so, inasmuch as the difficulty of arriving at truth seems to vary with the preciousness and refinement of its kind? I have observations on this at length in one of my University Sermons.

Is it not a coincidence (not to speak of the authority of Scripture declarations) that so much is said of "crying after wisdom," "asking and knocking" etc. etc. in Scripture?

When then a certain portion of our race are certain they have found religious truth, should we not feel as we might do, if while ignorant of mathematics, we found a number of educated persons simply confident of Newton's conclusions? I mean, admit that truth was attainable in religion, though *we* had not attained it.

Nor do I think it matters that many men are "certain" of what is opposite to Catholic truth—or "certain" that Catholicism is false—for men have been "certain" that Newton was false, yet that would not move me against Newton, because, though we are no judge of Newton's reasonings, we may be judges of the persons who use and embrace them, and all the Dominicans in the world might not move us in favor of anything *but* Newton's, though we understood the arguments on neither side. In like manner there are men *rationally* certain in religion—and irrationally certain,—and we may be judges of this, though not as yet judges of their reasons.

And here, recurring to what I said before, I do really think the character and variety of the converts to Catholicism of late in England form a most powerful argument, that there is such a thing as ascertainable truth in religion, and I am willing that a man should set against them, Luther, Cranmer, and Co., if he wishes.

Next it must be considered that, though there is a profession of certainty among Protestants, and pious earnest persons among them, yet their certainty commonly relates to, and their religious life is seated in, doctrines which are included in Catholicism. So that their certainty cannot be considered to contradict and invalidate the certainty of Catholics.

I do not think then, that any primâ facie incompleteness or unsatisfactoriness of the arguments for Catholicity are sufficient to lead me to acquiesce in the notion that truth cannot be attained about it.[7] For whatever probability there is, from the persons professing certainty about Catholicity, that they are rationally certain, such degree of probability is there that those arguments are *only* primâ facie and not substantial, of this incomplete and unsatisfactory character.

On the other hand, taking the two instances, to which W. F. refers, Keble is not certain of *any*thing—and if I put him on one side, and men like R. Wilberforce, Hope Scott, or Allies on the other, he does not pretend to collide with them; he only has not what they have.

Again, as to Pusey, he indeed is most " certain "—but the greater part of things [so] far, of which he is certain, are those of which Catholics are certain—and as to other points, in which he differs from Catholics, how he can be said to be certain of them I cannot tell, for, if his words are fairly quoted, he contradicts himself continually, or affirms to one person, what he denies to another.

Then, when, quitting this view of the subject, we fall back

---

[7] My argument is that against the probability adverse to Catholicism, arising from the *primâ facie* incompleteness of its proof, must be put the primâ facie probability in its behalf arising from the " certainty " of Catholics. [Newman's note.]

to the consideration of the arguments themselves, it must be recollected that in all departments *cuique in arte sua credendum*. By which I mean that, as I have said above, a man cannot suddenly get up a subject, and see the drift and bearings of it, the relative importance of its parts, and the value of its arguments.

Men who have lived in the dark, see things with a clearness unintelligible to those who enter it from the broad day. That religious truth is an obscure subject is granted; but that does not prove that we cannot find out its roads and their terminations.

We are told by Bishop Butler, that this difficulty of finding is the very trial of our earnestness, and the medium of our reward.

Every science requires a preparation, that we may feel and appreciate its principles and views. Is it unnatural that the subject of religion needs a preparation too?

Is it wonderful, if, considering religion is a special subject, this process should be peculiar? Is it wonderful, considering that its scope and its subject are supernatural, its preparation should be supernatural also?

Perhaps then what divines call grace, the supernatural assistance of the Father of Lights, may be the necessary preparation for our understanding the force of the arguments in the subject matter of religion; and perhaps prayer may be the human means, in the way of cause and effect, of gaining that supernatural assistance.

I do not see then that I am bound to believe W. F's statement of the unsatisfactoriness of religious inquiry, and the necessity of an everlasting suspense, until I am sure that he contemplates the probability of that being true, which is not improbable in itself, and which all those who have attained certainty say *is* true—that a preparation of mind of a particular kind is indispensable—for successful inquiry—and till he makes it clear to me that he duly appreciates that probability.

I should like an inquirer to say continually " O my God, I confess that *Thou* canst enlighten my darkness. I confess that Thou *only* canst. I *wish* my darkness to be enlightened. I do not know whether Thou wilt; but that Thou canst, and that I wish, are sufficient reasons for me to *ask*, what Thou at least has[t] not forbidden my asking. I hereby promise Thee that, by Thy grace which I am seeking, I *will embrace* whatever I at length feel certain is the truth, if ever I come to be certain. And by Thy grace I will guard against all self deceit which may lead me to take what nature would have, rather than what reason approves."

If a man tells me he has thus heroically cast himself upon God, and persisted in such a prayer, and yet is in the dark, of course my argument with him is at an end. I retire from the discussion and leave the matter to God. . .

In W. F's other letters there is a great deal which seems to me philosophical and deep, but it does not seem to bear, not to be meant to bear, on religion.

As to what he says of the difficulty of understanding one another's words, I don't suppose it applies to the above, which, according to my view of the subject, is engaged upon the root of the whole matter.

In 1851, when Newman wrote the letter given above, Froude was travelling in the Mediterranean, and in his letters home remarked upon the customs in the Catholic cathedrals on the continent. What particularly struck him, as on another occasion it had struck his brother Anthony, was the notice of Indulgences posted in the churches. Such bland legislation for the world beyond was to him laughably unreasonable. Mrs. Froude communicated his sentiments to Newman, and in doing so remarked upon the particular aspect which had so amazed her husband—the entire lack of written conditions (which every Catholic knew to be implicit) for the indulgence. In his reply Newman took just that lightness of tone natural to one brushing aside a misunderstanding so absurd as to be unworthy of serious attention.

Oratory B^m
Oct. 14/51.

My dear Mrs Froude,

I am not going into controversy—but I could not help smiling at your argument agst Indulgences from William's observation. I will give you a parallel. A Frenchman, who had travelled through England, said what struck him most, was the extreme munificence of the Inn keepers, he saw everywhere put up "Entertainment for man and horse"—not a word about paying. He had been told we were a nation of shopkeepers—but he never was so agreeably disappointed. He had never indeed entered an inn *himself,* but had slept sometimes in his travelling carriage, sometimes in friends' houses—but he could vouch for the fact—and he recorded it in a letter he sent home during his travels. In his next letter he added a further pleasing trait of character of a similar kind—viz. he found on every third door, as he walked through the private streets and squares of London, written, "Ring the bell." He had never indeed rung it, but *there* were the hospitable words, and they could not be explained away. . .

God bless you all, and believe me
Ever yours affect^ly
John H. Newman.
Congr. Orat.

Oratory B^m.
Oct. 20 1851.

My dear Mrs Froude,

I never can be hard upon you, whom I love so well, and it is a great shame you shd say so. I thought, in alluding to what Wm said, that no *conditions* were *mentioned* on the notice of Indulgence at Marseilles, that you concluded, "Therefore, the Wards are wrong, for they said there always *were* conditions." I answer "So *there* are—there are in that Marseilles one." You object, "They are not *written down*."

I reply "Certainly not, we do not write down what everyone takes for granted." Then followed my innocent parable, viz. it is *as* preposterous to suppose there are no conditions *because* they are not written down, as that there are no conditions to "Entertainment for man and horse," viz. *paying,* or for "Ring the Bell," viz. needing to call. Life wd not be long enough for it, if we put down in writing what everyone knew. And this was part of the subject treated in my 8th Lecture— viz. that to know the meaning of Forms (e. g.) of Indulgences, you must not go by what Hurrell used to call "textises" (texts) but, instead of fancying what *must* be, ask Catholics what *is*. I meant that the Ward's *assurance* was not at all impaired by William's *eyes*. What, dear Mrs Froude, is "hard" in this? As to the *theological* question I did not dream, nor do dream, of going into it. I said quite enough in former letters to show how I disapprove the plan of thinking that everything must be level to reason when you are called to a system of faith. The simple question is, "have I *reason enough* to resolve to place faith?" . . .

Ever yrs aff[ly]

J. H. Newman.

P. S. Do not suppose I have not ever the kindest and most considerate and loving thoughts of you.

In this same year, while Froude was absent on his travels, Newman was plunged into the harassment of the Achilli trial, the story of which is sufficiently well known to spare here an account of the disgraceful conduct of the prosecution and of Justice Coleridge in passing sentence upon the absurd verdict rendered by a dozen shopkeepers. It so happened that Froude was able to be of some small assistance by discovering in Italy information of value to the defense. The following notes give an indication of the secrecy and haste with which Newman had to prepare his case and of the loyalty with which his friends rallied to his support.

Oratory,
B^m.
Dec. 17 1851.

My dear Mrs Froude,

I had heard of W^m's kind zeal for me from my friends the Bowdens at Malta. It is strange that neither he nor John Bowden fell in with a Mr Larking Reynolds, who is helping us very energetically there, and who will go, either by himself, or with our lawyer Mr Hasting, to Corfu and Zante. *Keep his name secret,* except from W^m, for we have no confidence that the opposite party is not doing its utmost abroad in every place to thwart us.

I will add the name of some persons who can be used as *sources of information.* I do not know how long W^m stops in the Ionian Isles—but he had best, if possible, cooperate with our lawyer and Mr Reynolds, if they get there in time.

The time for affidavit is over. The judges would not give me a day to get affidavit in, tho' I am brought to trial on an affidavit of Achilli's. In spite of my counsel urging that they might be making the Court the tool of a perjurer, they refused me what would have enabled me to prove him so, on the pretence that I did not believe what I said, and was seeking, without knowing of evidence. My first legal notice of the proceedings ag[st] me was on October 27. They sent me to trial Nov[r] 21st thus allowing less than a month for getting a lawyer and communicating with Corfu, Malta and Italy—nay it was less than 3 weeks—for the matter did not come into Court till November 4.

However, the time of Affidavits is over—and nothing will do but witnesses in court, and they must distinctly bear witness, not to what they have heard, but to what they know personally.

The names I spoke of above are as follows:—

Father Pelagio Runi, Catholic Chaplain, Cepalonia.
Father Gerardini, Chaplain to Troops, Zante.
Dr Scandella, Malta.

With many thanks and all kind wishes.

Yrs affect[ly]
John H. Newman.

Oratory,
Bm.
Dec. 19/51.

My dear Mrs Froude,

There is one thing which William could do. We know Mr. Reynolds, late in the Police or Customs at Zante, to be a most respectable man—but of course our opponent[s] will be saying everything they can to impeach his motions etc. when he comes forward agst Achilli.

It would be a great gain if William could quietly get information about him, his relations to Government, to Achilli etc. that we may be prepared with *answers* to any attack on him.

Do not mention his name except to William.

Ever yrs aff^{ly}
John H. Newman.

Froude was among the many who contributed generously toward defraying the outrageous expenses to which Newman was put in his defence.

Edgbaston, B^m.
July 4 1852.

My dear William,

I got your letter last night here. Many thanks indeed for your munificent contribution, which took me by surprise, as you may think.

The sympathy which I am exciting is doing for me what success could not do in the way of clearing me of my expenses. They are frightful. Perhaps £6000—and, if Ld Campbell and Co can, some thousands in addition in behalf of the prosecutors. But I trust this will not be—it is bad enough as it is.

When they thought I should have difficulty in getting witnesses, they hurried on the Trial rudely and violently. When I was so prospered as to have my witnesses by Feb. 2, then they put it off to tire me out. I have had to keep them together for 6 months. . .

> Ever yrs aff^ly
> John H. Newman. . . .

> Edgbaston,
> Birmingham.
> July 4, 1852.

My dear Mrs Froude,

Your and William's letters followed me to Ireland, and then followed me back. I got them last night. You may fancy how acceptable they were.

Certainty is not the trial, but suspense, and I have had enough of it; but, with great thanks I say it, it is over. I do not think that fire and imprisonment will try me like suspense, especially since I am supported by the commonsense of mankind. . .

It touched me much to hear what you said of the Archdeacon, it showed both the goodness of my cause, and his latent kind feeling for me.

I know well that there is no one who has truer attachment to me than yourself—may God reward you.

> Ever yrs affect^ly
> John H. Newman.

Throughout these years, under Newman's quiet guidance, Mrs. Froude's sympathies for the Roman Catholic religion were steadily increasing, and the time was not far distant when she was to make formal confession of that faith. She continually addressed letters on religious subjects to Newman, frequently writing what amounted to " reports " on the general feeling of Anglicans toward the Roman Church. Newman as steadily pointed out, in the gentlest manner, the path of her duty.

16 Harcourt Street Dublin.
March 2, 1854.

My dear Mrs Froude,

Your kind congratulations [8] have just come to hand, having followed me over Ireland, through which I have been ranging. I *thought* you were thinking of me on the 21st and I did not forget you and William on the 28th, when my intention at Mass was the repose of the souls of Hurrell, Mr S. Wood, and my dear friend John Bowden, who, all three (humanly speaking) would have been Catholics, had they lived till now.

I grieve to hear you confirm what I have long felt, the mysterious antipathy of our population to Catholicism. The surplice controversy first clearly brought it out unless you say that Devonshire is more Protestant than the rest of England. I don't suppose that Hurrell or I had ever any *real* idea of the English *population* being influenced by Church principles—though sometimes doctrines may, in order to their elucidations, have been new and then thrown into the shape of anticipations—but certainly every event since 1833 has gone to show those, who would be Catholics, that they must come out of their own people as Abraham or St Paul. I forget minutely all that has passed between us, and may be saying what is inconsistent with, or a repetition, of what has been said before, but, My dear Mrs Froude, *do* you pray for " effectual grace "? Suppose I come to a high wall—I cannot jump it—such are the moral obstacles which keep us from the Church. We see the Heavenly City before us, we go on and on along the road, till a wall simply crosses it. Human effort cannot clear it, there is no scaling, no vaulting over. Grace enables me to cross it—and that grace is called effectual grace. Our first grace is sufficient to enable us to pray for that second effectual grace and God gives grace for grace.

Excuse this sermon, and with love to William and the dear child you brought to see me.

Ever yours affect[ly]

John H. Newman,

of the Oratory.

[8] On his fifty-third birthday. Newman was born February 21, 1801.

So marked now were Mrs. Froude's leanings toward Catholicism that her husband became seriously alarmed over her sentiments. He was too jealous of the intellectual freedom of an individual to attempt to persuade her against her leanings by other than purely logical exposition of the great mass of argument on the other side. He realized of course the full extent of Newman's influence over his wife and attempted to combat this by continuing to send argumentative letters to Newman. In 1854 he repeated in more elaboration what he had written in his letter of 1845 which had gone astray at Rome. Regrettably only a fragment of this survives among Newman's papers at Edgbaston, but it is clear from his reply that he was much interested in what Froude had written and that he had kept the letter for future use as he did others of Froude's communications. But from the few pages given below one may judge the temper of Froude's mind and the uneasiness with which he contemplated his wife's probable course.

You may remember that I told you I had written to you at Rome and that you had never received the letter—and this is it. If you have time to read it you will, I think, see that its arrival will have quickened any wish of mine to explain myself to you, not in the way of testifying, or as if what I had to say could be of any importance to you, or weigh with you, but because I always feel that your continued and unwearied warm and kind affection, makes some explanation,—some openness on my part—of the nature of a debt which I owe to you, and which (as this letter reminds me I needed to be reminded of it) I have often acknowledged and which I never can deny.

It seems safe enough—if not mean and cowardly to go on acknowledging debts when in the same breath, one admits the inability to pay. Yet such is my position and it is one which

I do not quite expect you to sympathize with—for you not long since told me it "was a paradox to say 'we (people in general) could not express our thoughts to each other in words'"—But the difficulty to me is a most real and serious one and seems the essence of almost all other difficulties, and a key to the position which on Religious questions my mind occupies.

I find it not less remarkably however in all questions, and its existence is most tangibly verified in cases where it ought to exist least—e. g. in questions of practical science—in which all men are agreed in the desirableness of making language the instrument of exact thought, and in which they have the greatest and most complete means which can exist anywhere of verifying and comparing meanings of words, and of expressions which are intended to convey modes of thought. I do not say that in questions of this kind words do not *help*, do not convey a *good deal* and set people on investigation etc., but dogmatic statements in these matters do fail absolutely to convey definite meanings or ideas, and to carry out (conclusively to others) the reasonings which they perhaps logically enclose. And on the other hand you will find that people agree precisely in their dogmatic statements on such questions, and yet in conversation and discussion it will come out perpetually that real differences lie hid beneath their words which no amount of talking will serve to clear up or dissipate. I do not wish to tempt you or to write a treatise on this difficulty. (By my own showing I should not understand it if you did so.) I only wish to let you know why I do not attempt an explanation which I admit to be of the nature of a debt, both in the way of duty and of affection.

But I must say something in reply to your kind letter about Kate. I had no scruple in showing it to her, and I am glad I did so for though I had before known pretty well the nature of the conflicts, thoughts and feelings, which govern her position, the conversation to which your letter gave rise, led me to see that I had not accurately struck the balance between them.

I fully believe that as far as reasonable or reasoning conviction goes, her judgment is against Catholicism—as far as feeling goes it is in favor—the feeling being partly what might be called fascination occasioned by the magnitude and endurance of the system, and what appears to her the adaptations of its ceremonial to her own peculiar turn of mind and partly her entire love and admiration for the catholics she has known—a love and admiration which goes entirely beyond that which she feels for any other persons whatever.

My conversations with her have led me to see that I have, if anything, underrated the force of the fascination, and it would not surprise me if it were some day or other wholly to outweigh all opposing forces of whatever kind.

I cannot say that such a result would not be painful to me and perhaps the knowledge which she would naturally have that the result would be painful to me, being of the same description to a certain extent, as those which load the opposite scales, would to a certain extent, steady the beam: with this exception no obstacle to her progress would occur on my part, for indeed I should have none else to offer, at least of a nature commensurable with the force of those springs which push her forward.

You will readily understand I am sure that it is with no very cheerful feelings that I contemplate as almost a probable result, a change which, though it could not impair affection, would in its very nature make an end of that full community of thought and judgment in which affection has had such scope.

I cannot trust myself to think or speak of it.

Yours affectionately,
W. Froude.

Newman fully appreciated the distress Froude suffered, a distress, moreover, that was to increase when, within a few years, his children too were to follow their mother into the Catholic Church. Fears of just this sort of thing had been partly responsible for the hesitation

WILLIAM FROUDE

Newman felt before his own conversion. He appears to have made some gesture toward discontinuing his correspondence with Mrs. Froude after he learned how severe a trial was being inflicted on William. He wrote:

> Oratory Edgbaston.
> April 10, 1854.
>
> My dear William,
>
> . . . Thank you very much for your long letter, and the inclosure. I have not forgotten the one you wrote me about a year ago—and have it safe in the desk I am writing on. If I did not answer it, it was not that I did not feel interest in it—and I shall read most anxiously what you now send.
>
> God ever bless you, my dearest William, I know I don't pray for you and your wife near so much as I ought.
>
> Ever yours most affect^{ly}
> John H. Newman.
>
> P. S. Let me add, that Catholics hold it would be wrong in any one becoming a Catholic without his *judgment* being convinced. This you know. At the same time you know my writings well enough (e. g. my University Sermons) to understand, that, at least in my opinion, persons may have very good reasons, which they cannot bring out into words. Your dear wife has said she would not write to me again—and I assure you, my dearest William, I shall not write to her—but you can't hinder me (nor wish to hinder me) praying, whatever the prayers are worth. . . .

So great was Newman's solicitude for Mrs. Froude's welfare, however, that he did not cease to write to her in his usual vein, though at the same time he was careful to insist that she communicate all that he had said to her husband. A month after Froude's letter Newman wrote again:

My dear Mrs Froude,
May 5, 1854.

I have been to England for a day and found your letter, and brought it with me here where I have just arrived and now sit down to thank you for it and the former one.

Be sure I shan't forget you and Wm please God. I shall for some time give my Friday's mass (excepting the 26th inst) to that intention.

Do not fancy you can put me in a painful position to dear Wm. I don't mind differing with him. I don't mind giving you advice in which he would not concur. But I wish to be sure I tell him so when I do it. He is so true and tender, but I leave you safely to him. But I never can disguise from him what I think and feel about you.

As to your reference to my letters, of course I may forget about myself—but just consider, since you have them with you, whether I am not right in saying, that I never was in doubt what *my duty was*. I doubted what was true, but I used to say " To join the church of Rome would be against my conscience. I *could not* do it." I don't say this was not a false conscience, but a conscience it *was,* and it is ever right to go according to one's conscience, though a false one.

Moreover, it is a Catholic principle that no one can be in doubt what he ought to *do* (i. e. without fault). We are often left " speculatively " doubtful, and use the theological word, never " practically." Shortly before my reception, when my book was partly printed,[9] I saw I *ought* to be a Catholic, and I did not then wait till I had finished the printing, but left the book unfinished, as it stands.

When my dear friend Bowden lay dead, I wept bitterly over his body, saying he had gone, and left me without light; this was the same feeling as far as I recollect. I don't think I was remaining a Protestant, thinking I ought *not* to remain, but with a sense of duty that I *ought* to remain *till* I got clear light.

I am not defending myself, but I am writing with reference to you, my dear Mrs Froude. See then whether your doubt

---

[9] *Development of Christian Doctrine.*

be merely speculative. Can you say "I am certain I ought now and here, at this time and place, to remain a Protestant"? Are you sure that, whatever remaining *speculative* doubts or difficulties you may have, you have not a secret feeling that you ought to be a Catholic? I am not attempting to answer this question *for* you, but I really cannot help having an opinion on the subject.

I hope I make this clear, but am somewhat anxious lest I should not.

Ever yrs aff[ly]

J. H. N.

Within two more years Mrs. Froude's mind was so convinced of the truth of Roman Catholicism that her reception awaited only the settling of practical details. Of these, however, there were not a few. It was feared that the Archdeacon, now nearly ninety years old and still as staunchly Anglican as in the days when he too was something of a Tractarian, might so seriously object to his daughter-in-law's becoming a Catholic as to cut off William as he had Anthony from his inheritance. This consideration, and the knowledge of the great pain William would feel at her conversion, for some time kept Mrs. Froude back. She wrote to Newman to see whether it might not be possible to become a Catholic and still attend the Anglican services merely to please and comfort the Archdeacon. Newman wrote for an official ruling on the unusual request but found that it was "peremptorily refused." The following letters give an account of the difficulties as they were finally resolved.

6 Harcourt Street,
Dublin.
April 24, 1856.

My dear Mrs Froude,

When I got your letter the other day, I said Mass at once

for you and William. I did not answer it at once, but now a second comes, I write. Nothing that I have ever written, as you know, do I not write for him as well as for you.

I do believe the dear Archdeacon's difficulty will be got over. You need be no trouble to him at all, I am sure.

Be sure I constantly think of you and William. These trials are like bad operations, but with fortitude and the grace of God we get through them.

> Ever yours aff^{ly}
> John H. Newman
> of the Oratory.

P. S. Don't think I write coldly, you may be sure I don't *feel* so. And you may be sure I never separate the thought of William from you, and never can be unmindful of much he undergoes, or with what sweet gentleness.

> The Oratory, Hagley Road,
> Birmingham.
> May 20/56.

My dear Mrs Froude,

May God reward you, as He will, for all your trials, and your resolute struggle under them. As to your answers to William's objections, no one could make better. As to the expression of them in words, every one must feel how difficult this is. He beyond others will and must, because his great difficulty, or rather obstacle, in writing to me was, that he could not do himself justice upon paper.

If you had acted hastily, impetuously, doggedly, without listening to others, that might have been a fair objection to you; but *you* surely are the best judge of your own reasons, and you have tested them by a long course of years.

The absolute certainty of faith in the truth of what the Church conveys to you from God, is the reward, through divine grace, of those souls who, before receiving it, have exercised their mental powers to the best; and you must throw yourself, in regard to it, on the Power, Love, and Faithfulness of Him who calls you.

You need not believe any thing that the Pope says, except when he speaks ex cathedrâ. His chance sayings need not be better than another man's, nor his measures in detail. I believe there were great corruptions all over Europe, before the rise of Protestantism; but I am very doubtful if much can be proved against the Pope's measures.

Since you distinctly ask me, I have no right to keep from giving you my distinct judgment, that you are bound to join the Church at once.

Ever yours affect^{ly},
with much anxiety for you,
John H. Newman.

God support you.

The Oratory B^m
Sept 13/56.

My dear Mrs Froude,

It so happens I wrote to Wm only yesterday on a matter of business.

I most sincerely congratulate you on your sister's reception. I have a dear young friend at Westbury, whom I baptized as a child, Mary Anne Bowden, in religion Sister Dominica.

As to yourself, of course, as you say, you must get William's leave—but, with it, I should certainly recommend your being received privately. It is one of those extreme cases, in which it is allowable. Of course the Bishop alone could give leave—Dr Vaughan; you would be much struck with him, if you knew him. Perhaps you do, at Clifton. However, the late Synods and the Hierarchy have made some alterations on these points. If William approved of it, I would make inquiry; or you could in your own way, through the nuns at Westbury etc. . . .

I am most thankful to say, I am quite well.

Ever yours affect^{ly}
John H. Newman
of the Oratory.

November 30, 1856.

(To Mrs. Froude)

One more thing I will say, gravely. I cannot, alas, deny that the fact that you will believe that dear Wm is "out of the pale of salvation," for that he will be, *whatever may be said to prove his case an exception,* for the burden of proof will be on his proving it, I say this cannot help leading you to be *most* desirous of his conversion. I never wish any of my letters not shown to him.

Ever yrs aff^{ly}

John H. Newman.

Dublin
Dec. 12, 1856.

(To Mrs. Froude)

No one can more dislike your being privately received than I—but the question is, What is to be done else? I *think* you might be allowed to go to the Protestant service, (so that you did not communicate) and family prayers. Shall I ask your Bishop? without of course giving him any clue who the inquirer is. As to its being hypocritical to go to Protestant worship, if the worship was Unitarian or Anti-Catholic, that would be another matter. There is nothing wrong in the Prayer. To remain at home, still professing to be a Protestant, would be quite as hypocritical—and a bad example to Protestants into the bargain.

So much as to abstract principles—but I do not know what the *rule* is.

In what state is Mrs Anthony Froude now? They say she is a Catholic still. Is it so?

Ever yrs aff^{ly}

J. H. N.

The Oratory Birmingham
Christmas Day 1856.

My dear Mrs Froude,

A happy Christmas to you and all yours. I have just received the Bishop's answer. It is in the negative. He says that the Pope did not give permission even to James the second to attend the Protestant service even for a short time. He " peremptorily refused." At the same time certainly in a missionary country much has been allowed. Confessors have had powers of their own, and on their own discretion have used them more freely than Bishops dare—for a Bishop's act is a precedent. Confessors have not such great powers since the coming in of the University.

The Bishop of Plymouth wants to know what he can do for you. He says he shall think of you especially now at Christmas, and recommend you, for the grace of courage, to our Infant Lord and God. I don't know what he can do more. And this is every thing.

As for me, I will say Mass for you next Sunday, and still, for the grace of courage.

The Bishop says he could give you for a while a dispensation from going to Mass on Sundays. Whether you will think this a gain, I don't know. For me, I think it *would* be a scandal your going no where, and the poor people would rather you went to Mass than that.

But you are the judge.

I end as I began. A happy, and blessed Christmas to you all, and, as the Angels say, peace to men of *good will*.

Ever yrs aff^{ly}

J. H. N.

6 Harcourt Street Dublin.
Feb. 20/57.

My dear Mrs Froude,

I have been anxiously thinking of you ever since I last heard from you.

I will write to Fr Johnson (who is he? a Jesuit?) and will urge your case as strongly as I can—but I don't know what he *can* do.

Ever yrs aff^{ly}

J. H. N.

Mrs. Froude was received into the Roman Catholic Church on the morning of March 19, 1857. She wrote at once to Newman:

>Convent of Mercy—Bristol
>March 19, 1857.

My dear sir,

I know that you will be glad to hear that I was received into the Catholic Church this morning. It is strange to think that you are the only person whom I now venture to tell of the great blessing which God has given me—not even my dearest W^m. I cannot say how grateful I feel to God for having helped me and supported me so wonderfully. But my heart aches for *him;* for he is miserable at the idea of our virtual separation—and he has nothing to fall back on whereas I could not be unhappy if I tried, even with all my sorrow for him.

. . . I must tell you how from my heart I thank you for what you have done to help me—other Catholics always seemed " making a case " when they said things to me—you always contrived to say exactly what suited my mind.

>6 Harcourt Street
>Dublin
>March 21, 1857.

My dear Mrs Froude,

You may fancy what joy your letter gave me. You will be sustained by the blessings and the graces which will surround you in the great trials which you may undergo. But every thing will be made light to you—and you must gain your husband by your prayers. . . .

>Ever yrs aff^{ly} in Xt,
>John H. Newman
>of the Oratory.

IV
CORRESPONDENCE THROUGH JANUARY, 1860

IV

CORRESPONDENCE THROUGH JANUARY, 1860

NEWMAN'S correspondence did not cease upon Mrs. Froude's conversion; he continued to send letters of sympathy and understanding during the time of spiritual adjustment which had naturally to follow upon her new belief. Before long his chief solicitude, and Mrs. Froude's, became the conversion of the children, Hurrell, Robert Edmund, Elizabeth, and Mary, and if possible, William himself, to the Roman Church. William remained an agnostic until his death, but it was a time of severe trial to him when his children one by one fell away under the influence of Newman and their mother. Only a single daughter, Mary, remained a Protestant, and by a cruel turn of fate she died in childhood. Two sons, Hurrell and Edmund, were received by Newman in 1859 and 1863, and thus Froude's spiritual isolation became almost complete. His solace was in his scientific experiments which were to prove so fruitful, and into these he plunged with renewed industry. He greatly feared lest belief in the Roman Catholic religion should give to his sons' minds a turn incompatible with scientific investigation, and it was consequently a source of real joy to find that his fears had been groundless and that both sons, even in youth, displayed considerable aptitude in the field of practical science. Shortly after going down from Oxford, Hurrell went out to India on an engineering project, while Edmund remained at home to assist his father in pioneer work on the motions of floating bodies.

Froude's affection for his family was never impaired

even under these trying circumstances, and he gradually became accustomed to the situation. He continued to talk freely on religious questions and to point out what seemed to him insuperable objections to the Roman Catholic belief. He fancied that his arguments had made some impression upon the religious views of Edmund, who now, from close association with his father, had acquired the habit of weighing and judging evidence in a scientific manner, and he rejoiced at these signs of his son's " tough mindedness," feeling that it augured great things for the future.

It may be imagined, then, how great was the shock when Froude suddenly learned that Edmund contemplated giving up science to become a priest. His distress was not unappreciated by Newman, who never more than on this occasion displayed his genius for entering into another's mind. He at once discouraged Edmund from taking up a vocation for which he readily recognized him to be unfitted. In the end Edmund returned to his father's laboratory further to assist in important experiments which later led to his own election to the Royal Society.

It was in the correspondence of the early 'sixties that Froude exerted his greatest influence over the mind of Newman. The problems he brought forward for discussion were personally important to him in view of his family situation, and he put forth his arguments with the utmost vigor and sincerity though at the same time in the most temperate of language. For a short time after his wife's conversion, however, he did not discuss religious questions with the intensity of a few years later. The relations of Newman and the Froudes proceeded for a while in quiet fashion. Newman's short letters at this time, written during the press of much work, give an intimate view of that mind which ran to such great depth. There is in them no suggestion of the brilliant dialectician who was shortly to raise his gigantic stature to crush utterly the toughest-minded of the Protestant clergy. Nor is there either any suggestion of a wily and sinister proselytizer, the "Romish intriguer" of popular fiction and fancy; there is only a sympathetic, devout English gentleman performing earnestly and humbly what he knew to be the will of God. The following notes show the delicacy with which he moved in the lives of Mrs. Froude and her children.

The Oratory, B^m.
Oct. 28/57.

My dear Mrs Froude,

It is a great comfort to receive and read your letters, and all that you tell me about yourself, and your children.

I did not know dear Isy's [1] direction, and answered through sister Dominica. At the same time I think it best not to correspond with her without her father's knowing—and you must not be disappointed, if, for a like reason, I think it best not to write to Hurrell.[2] God will hear your prayers, and bring about your wish in some way known to Himself. What you said about him has interested me extremely.

I am going to Ireland in a day or two, and shall be there for about three weeks.

Ever yours aff^{ly} in Xt
John H. Newman
of the Oratory.

The O^y B^m
Dec. 11, 1857.

My dear Mrs Froude,

Thank you very much for your interesting and pleasant, though painful, details. You have been brought forward

[1] E. M. Froude (the late Baroness Anatole von Hügel).
[2] Froude's son.

wonderfully, and will be brought through. I am very glad you are so open with William, and am sure he will understand the value of it. He will understand how great a thing it is to rely with full confidence that there is nothing unknown to him. What you say about Hurrell is very hopeful—but, while you pray as if immediate success were likely, you must not be cast down at disappointment. There seems a great prospect of your winning them both at last—but you must persevere.

Thank you for letting me see dear Hurrell's letter.

Ever yours aff^{ly} in Xt
John H. Newman,
of the Oratory.

Newman always said he got on splendidly with younger men but not with older ones. He had a genius for leading forward younger minds, a genius which, had it been again free in Oxford, might have started a second great religious movement. The ease with which he put himself on a level with his correspondent without at the same time sacrificing dignity or influence may be seen in a charming light letter he sent to young Hurrell Froude, who at the time was entertaining most romantically exaggerated views of the confessional.

Oratory B^m August 11/57.

Charissime,

I should have written to you by the first post .... were I not in such a suffocation of business, from the lectures I am delivering. And now I cannot say much more than express my thankfulness to Him who has brought you so far, and will surely bring you on still. Your ideas about Confession are most unreal and romantic. The Priest is nothing, God is every thing. They are the greatest friends who know each other most intimately. The Confessor's sympathy so flows out upon a penitent that it is as if he were making, not hearing a Confession. I can only repeat, you are making bugbears.

WILLIAM FROUDE 113

What I should *like* would be, if you could come and live with us for a week, pledged to nothing. You would see Catholicism to a disadvantage so much as this, that we profess nothing. We have nothing high about us—you would be sharp enough to see this. We do not profess it—what we profess is to do hard work for the sake of Christ—to be busy, and to be cheerful. You might see things to shock you—never mind. I want nothing hid from you. It would try you—if you overcame it, it would be a test to you, where your heart lay and what was God's will. If your romantic idea continued, Charissime, I would not quarrel with it—but send you up—if you were disposed to the Cistercian Convent at Mount St Bernard, where every one wears a white habit, and fasts till 12 or 1 in the day—and whom you need never see again. Charissime, pardon and forget it, if I seem to be light. Here am I worked beyond my powers, just now; but if you would bring work, you could mix with us naturally, tho' no one has time on his hands. On Friday or Saturday comes a French architect with suggestions for a Basilica, and our own architect who is of your own trade, being the Engineer on the Blackbarn Rail. Tres faciunt Collegium. We should be sure to have a good plan, if you joined them.

Write to me, please, and say you forgive me, if I have written freely.

Ever yrs affectionately
John H. Newman
Congr. Orat.

P. S. I said Mass for you directly your letter came.

Newman could step down easily to even younger minds. Isy Froude, then a young child, also had her important questions to ask in regard to her future course, and she too confided in Newman more readily than in any one else, and to her Newman wrote a gentle note urging her to do nothing precipitantly, but to talk openly with her father.

Dublin
Oct. 29/58.

My dear Child,

I have just got your letter. Since I saw you, I have been remembering you in my prayers several times a day,—you and your brother especially.

I think it would be good, as you propose, to offer to let Papa talk to you—but you must pray God earnestly before it, and during the conversation, for grace to do in all things His holy will.

I think your letter is a very natural one, and therefore a very good one. I think you *should* send one.

And now I believe I have answered your questions, though I am writing in a hurry to save the post.

Ever yours affect[ly]
John H. Newman.

The correspondence took shortly a more serious turn. On Christmas Eve, 1859, Hurrell, the oldest son, then eighteen, was received into the Roman Catholic Church. Newman wrote to Froude a letter which in its very abruptness was kind. It was composed with great deliberation, and a copy which he preserved for himself is so full of blots and interlinings, whether from the emotion of the subject or not, as to be scarcely decipherable.

Dec. 24, 1859.

My dear Wm,

I have this day received Hurrell into the Catholic Church . . . It was his own proposal, I believe, to come here and I gave my consent. He mentioned his intention to the Donkins [a] as long as ten days ago.

With my convictions I could do nothing else. Till I saw

---

[a] William Fishburn Donkin (1814-1869), from 1842, the Savilian professor of Astronomy at Oxford.

some of his letters and at length saw himself, I doubted very much whether he showed evidence of firm purpose, which would warrant me in receiving him. I thought he might be in the power of a fancy which would die away. I had no wish at all as you will surely believe me to take advantage of a boy's chance humour. The most careful judgment indeed may be at fault, or anticipate wrongly; but, certainly unless I felt there was a real prospect of his perseverance, I shouldn't have received him.

As to yourself, I do not believe, I never will believe, that in the bottom of your mind you really hold what you think you hold, or that you master your own thoughts. I think that some day you will allow the truth of what I say. Accordingly, whatever pain it is to me to think of our actual differences of opinion, I feel no separation [from] you in my heart, I, please God, never shall.

H. N.

To Froude the news came at a particularly difficult moment. His father, the old Archdeacon, had recently died, and his son's formal confession of intellectual principles so at variance with all that he held most sacred brought the feeling of a great additional loss. And then, too, the very times were stirring, filled with new ideas and beliefs tending more and more to diverge from Catholic principles. There was then a spirit afloat as there had been in the Tract days, but of a very different sort, a scientific spirit making great advances, stirring up the ferment which was to mark yet another epoch in modern thought. Darwin's book had just been published; the following year was to bring forth another scarcely less influential, *Essays and Reviews,* written in part by some of Froude's own associates. In this movement of modern scientific thought, Froude himself held a distinguished place, and hoped to see his sons carry forward his speculations. It was, therefore, impossible for him not to feel that Hurrell, in joining the Roman Catholic Church, was renouncing all that promised best for the future and giving over his intellectual freedom and integrity for a faith which could at most offer mere peace of mind, and even that only to those satisfied never to inquire.

There was nothing in either Newman's letter or his action to which Froude felt it possible to object, but the occasion seemed to be a fitting one on which to offer an apologia for his own beliefs. Hence the long letter he sent in reply was in a manner a summation of his thought since the Oxford days. Remarkable even for its literary style, the letter gives a statement, probably as succinct as any in existence, of those principles of thinking and investigating which actuated the best of the liberal minds of the mid-nineteenth century. Much of it appears today as truisms, but one has only to search out passages on a similar theme, in Huxley's writing, for example, to recall how far from general acceptance was this attitude of mind at the time. The letter is particularly pertinent as showing how Froude's criticism helped to shape Newman's further thought, for in it the weakest points of Newman's philosophy are laid bare under a penetrating and strictly reasonable analysis.

Elmsleigh, Paignton, Torquay.
29th Dec. 1859.

My dear Newman,

I must at least thank you for your most kind letter. I am well aware that with your conviction, you couldn't have done otherwise than you have done in reference to Hurrell. Nor could I for a moment have supposed that you were likely to encourage anybody, least of all, one in whom you felt a special interest, in becoming a convert, where there was not a prospect of real perseverence.

No one, I think, who has ever enjoyed the privilege of affectionate intercourse with you can fail to experience a sense of acute pain on coming to feel that he has become practically severed from you, in whatever way the severance has arisen. Rogers [4] has always said it was, to him, "like losing a limb," and I know of no expression which has so accurately described my own feeling. There remains of course the consciousness of the persistent affection with which you regard me. And those who are near me lay great stress on this, and say if it be so with you, a portion of it may be and ought to be so with them. And they seem to think it strange that the maintenance thus of mutual affection between me and them should leave room for the unhappiness which they see I experience in the circumstances in which we are placed. I neither disregard, nor I believe, do I undervalue such affection, but for my own part, ever since I began to think at all, and still more markedly in my later years, I have felt (and if I rightly understand the latter part of your letter you will agree with me in the feeling far more than those do who are more near to me) that the sort of unitedness to which one gives the name of "affection" must be called valueless when compared with that which consists in the unity of judgment and unity of aim, in reference to all those deeper questions which are proper to our life when considered as something better than a mere animal existence—valueless, comparatively, because incommensurable, or as a mathematician would say "for a lower order" a figure for the surfaces which bound a solid, not the solid itself, and thus a source of pain rather than a comfort by perpetually reminding one of that solid which ought to fill the space, and keeping alive a craving which it does not tend to satisfy. And so it happened that long ago when I found my mind diverging from the track you had laid down, and settling into views widely at variance with your's, what I most desired was to have your solution of the difficulties which had thrown me off into the new direction. It has perhaps seemed to you that I have made but little effort to accomplish this—but this ap-

[4] Frederick Rogers, Lord Blachford.

pearance, at the outset, grew out of your non reply to a letter (occasioned as it afterwards turned out by your not having received it) which I wrote to you at Rome, and since that time you may perhaps recollect, on several occasions I have gone to you, and written to you, with a more or less definite object of explaining my own course of thought and of learning how it would be acted on by discussion with you. And though whatever has passed on these occasions may have been slight, so slight perhaps as to have made little impression on your memory, yet the result has in every case been to strengthen, not to weaken my confidence in the path I have been pursuing.

It may indeed be as you tell me that I " do not really hold what I seem to hold," and " do not master my own views "—but to me it seems as if, different as are many of my opinions (if indeed I can be said to hold positive opinions) from those you would teach me, there is underlying all such differences, and irrespective of them or undercutting them, a source of disagreement between us indefinitely stronger than they, seated in the very principle of "thinking" and of "concluding" and in the very nature of thoughts and of conclusions—and pervading the laws, which govern the various states of mind included in the various senses of the term " belief," and which fix the duties attached to them.

In reference to these subjects, my convictions so to call them, are the growth of a life, I seem to hold them or be held by them, very completely, and to see my way through them as clearly as I can see my way through anything—they first were reared, I am confident, under the mental training I received from my Brother Hurrell, and I am persuaded they have since been legitimately developed. The substance of their nourishment has been derived chiefly from the circumstances of active life which have operated on them the more directly and more forcibly from the fact that they have lain so much in the domain of practical science, where, more than elsewhere, the principles and results of reasonings are confronted with the test of direct experiment, and where to be divested of prejudices and to arrive at truth simply, is the object most directly before the eyes, and is less difficult to pursue straight forward, than in any other departments of thought. By slow—(but only by slow) degrees the convictions I refer to become masters of my whole mind, mastering the dogmatic habit of thought, first in its relation to professional knowledge and scientific enquiry, (for when I was an undergraduate the general tone of Oxford teaching was at least as dogmatic in relation to sciences as in relation to Theology and had laid strong hold on me, there), and then penetrating at length into the region of Theology and altering my views in reference to it, so as to produce results which I fully admit to be at variance with Hurrell's direct teaching.

That in preference to the conclusions which he had drawn from his principles of thought, I should adhere to those which I have myself drawn from them, exposes me, I admit to the charge of presupposition. And in reply to this all I have to say (and what in part at least satisfies me) is, that his own mind was, as he himself felt, in many respects in a state of transition, and it is at least possible that he should have arrived at the same conclusions as those at which I have arrived, and there are many reasons which incline me to think he would have done so. But the consciousness that this surmise may be an error, does not at all shake my confidence that the principles of thought by which I am guided are not merely those which the experience of life has fully verified to me, but are also those which he was the first to develop in my mind.

I have no skill of saying much in few words and the profusion of words into which I sum my thoughts tends oftener to mystify than to explain. But I will at least endeavour to convey to you as distinctly as I can that rule or principle of thought which (irrespective of all differences of opinion) seems to hold my mind in the most complete antagonism to Catholicism. More strongly than I believe anything else I believe this—that no subject whatever—distinctly not in the region of the ordinary facts with which our daily experience is consonant—distinctly not in the domain of history or of politics, and yet again a fortiori, not in that of Theology, is my mind, (or as far as I can take the mind of any human being,) capable of arriving at an absolutely certain conclusion. That though of course some conclusions are far more certain than others, there is an element of uncertainty in all.

That though any probability however faint, may in its place make it a duty to *act as if* the conclusion to which it points were absolutely certain, yet that even the highest attainable probability does not justify the mind in discarding the residuum of doubt; and that the attempt (by any other means than a reiterated and (if [it] be improved) examination of all the bases of the whole probability) to enhance or intensify the sense of the preponderance of the probabilities in either scale, is distinctly an immoral use of faculties. And then, whereas on concluding that it is one's duty to act on such and such a degree of probability (whether great or small) the mind is very strongly drawn and inclined, to overrate the degree of probability in reference to which we proceed to act, this inclination is a temptation to be resisted, not an intimation to be relied on.

But when with integrity of heart anyone is conscious that he has done his very best to arrive at a true conclusion, whether by careful examination of the facts and investigation of their relations or by taking the advice of them, though he is not only bound to be guided in his conduct by such a conclusion but also ought to be "confident" that this is, for him, "the best" and "to have faith" in his cause, it is at the same time not less religiously his duty to keep before his eyes his knowledge of the fallibility of his processes of thought and those of advisers, and to maintain as vivid a recollection of the probabilities which lie against his conclusion, however small they may seem, as of the preponderating mass of probabilities in favor of it—And instead of saying "this is my honest belief and so help me God it ever shall be"—he ought to say "this is for the present the best conclusion I can come to, but in the sight of God I declare that I shall be at all times ready to reconsider it, if reasonably called on to do so, either in the score of errors of fact, or errors of judgment. Nay, I shall be anxious to reconsider it, exactly in proportion as I have grave reason to expect that honest reconsideration will lead me to abandon it." Our "doubts" in fact appear to me as *sacred,* and I think deserve to be cherished as sacredly as our beliefs; and our "will" has no function in reference to the formation or maintenance of our "Belief," but that of insisting that all probabilities on either side shall be honestly regarded, and weighed and borne in mind.

You will therefore readily understand that the fixedness of purpose with which Hurrell [5] has taken this step does not, to me at least, convey an enhanced impression of the soundness of judgment or the rightness of mind evinced by it. Had he been steering his boat at a regatta with baffling winds and intricate tides, or had he been riding a steeplechase in difficult country, and judged that he should do better by "taking a line of his own" than by sticking to the course which he had been originally taught to follow—then if in taking the line he had said to himself "Though I think I see my way clearly, it is nevertheless possible that I may be wrong, I will therefore continue to be on the look-out for whatever may show whether I have been right or wrong" and had he said this with an honest intention of as readily admitting a proof that he had been wrong as of being satisfied he had been right—I think my brother Hurrell would have said (as I say) that thus and thus only he has wisely given effect to the dictum "To us, probability is the very guide of life."

When then, in starting on the race of life, he sets out by choosing his own line, the fact that he chooses it without misgiving and without reservation, impresses me the more unfavorably, in proportion as the stakes are more important and the choice of a course turns on considerations more really difficult of solution.

I do not overlook the view that "Spiritual insight is granted as the reward of Faith," nor do I venture to judge that (in some shape) it is an impossible or even an improbable one. Yet I feel it to be one in the highest degree improbable if

---

[5] Froude's son.

the merit of Faith be measured as the Theologians seem to measure it, directly as the *positiveness* of the Belief and inversely *as the strength* of the evidence. Thus measured Faith seems to be but another word for " prejudice "—i. e., as the formation of a judgment, irrespective of, or out of proportion to the evidence on which it rests and I regard it as an instance of an immoral temper or an immoral use of the faculties. While on the other hand the only pattern of Faith which I can conceive to be meritorious, is the temper which, while it realizes as carefully as possible the exact degree of doubtfullness which attaches to its conclusions, *acts* nevertheless confidently on the best and wisest conclusion it can form— in confidence that the best and wisest use of every faculty we possess must be that use which will be most pleasing to Him by whom these faculties, whether perfect or imperfect, have been given us " to be exercised therewith."

It is but of late years that this temper has been thoroughly appreciated in the pursuit of scientific truth and in the cultivation of the mechanical arts, though here, earlier than elsewhere, its want was felt, and there were fewest obstacles to its growth. Its *thorough* appreciation however, even in these departments of thought seems confined to the higher class of minds (if I feel that it is pretty thoroughly appreciated by myself, I attribute it to the peculiar manner in which the development of principles first cultivated in my mind by Hurrell was assisted and disentangled by my interview[s] with Brunel—a man of singular grasp of thought, and truthfulness and honesty of purpose, and whose views have often seemed to me to be most remarkably supplemental to or explanatory of Hurrell's). And if year by year, Physical science and the mechanical arts, have of late, made progress with increasing rapidity and security, it is only by virtue of the wider and freer scope of action which this principle has conquered for itself in those districts of thought. The principle is making some progress even in Politics. Bye and bye I hope it will master men's minds in the province of religion.

For myself, in every province of thought and action, I am content to take as my motto the words " Ever learning and never able to come to a knowledge of the Truth." So long as I am able honestly to claim for myself the former characteristic, I am ready to submit contentedly to the reproach (if anyone choose to consider it a reproach) implied in the latter as a condition inherent in imperfect faculties—I will not bury the talent in the earth on the plea that the Master " is a hard one and gathers when he has not strewed."

You tell me indeed that " I do not really hold what I seem to hold, nor master my own thoughts "—and you say that some day or other I shall admit the truth of the observation— so be it! it is my principle to catch at any honest proof that I am in error and whenever you will help me to accomplish this, the reversal of my fundamental principle of universal doubt, it shall honestly exert its last effort on itself, in virtue of itself it shall destroy itself, and shall commit suicide when it has landed me at the threshold of certainty. But till that is accomplished, the principle would continue to hold me in universal scepticism, were you to show me and were I to admit, and act on the admission, that there is an enormously preponderating probability of the truth of every proposition of Catholic Theology.

Do not think I am vain enough to suppose my words will make the faintest trace of an impression on your mind; but I have owed it to you these long years past, to say something of, and for, myself. If my thoughts were less unready than they are to shape themselves into words, if when I have made the effort to express them, I could feel a rational hope that the words would convey them substantially to another mind as they exist in my own,—if the effort were less painful to me, painful from its laboriousness and its helplessness and doubly painful from its pressure on all the home troubles and division with which the thoughts are interwoven, I should long since have endeavoured to acquit myself of the debt. As it is though my letter has been a long one, I feel at the end of it that I might as well have let the occasion pass in sorrowful silence or with a bare acknowledgment of the kindness of your letter—but that so curt a reply (or still more) silence, might have implied sulkiness or cowardice.

Do not trouble yourself to write a long answer to this letter—indeed I dare say you will feel you can dispose of it in a very few words—and at all events, I know how fully your time is occupied.

> Believe me, yours affectionately,
> W. Froude.

Froude's letter clearly stated the issues as they were drawn by scientists. Newman was among the very few in the Roman Catholic Church who appreciated the depth of the scientific argument and the extreme urgency of meeting it if the cause of religion were not to suffer additional setbacks at the hands of the liberals. The problem was by no means a superficial one but rather seated, as Froude said, " in the very principle of ' thinking ' and of 'concluding,' and in the very nature of thoughts and conclusions—and pervading the laws which govern the various states of mind included in the various senses of the term ' belief,' and which fix the duties attached to them." The problem was of course no new one, but the consequences likely to follow upon a failure to solve it were of more serious moment than they had been before.

It is of some interest to note that the thought of these two men had a common source and for a time a common direction. Both had as their point of departure Butler's *Analogy*, and both had been familiar with and influenced by Hurrell Froude's interpretation of " To us, probability is the guide of life." Hurrell was notably unafraid of inferences, as Hugh James Rose remarked on the occasion of the famous meeting at the Hadleigh Rectory in 1833. Hurrell had instilled his principle of thinking in William at an early age, and William frequently acknowledged his indebtedness. Newman too had come under this influence, but of the two it was not Newman but William Froude who seems to have adhered most strictly to Butler's dictum, for the whole success of his life's work depended upon nice distinctions between the more and less probable, upon determining, as often as possible by actual experiment, the exact strength of the probability in question. Froude's mind reacted to evidence with a precision from which every trace of emotion, prejudice, or preconception had been rigidly excluded. Newman on the contrary deviated from this clear line and brought from his own mind certain additional elements, and those quite imponderable, which frequently became the ruling factors in his decisions. Thus, though relying upon probabilities, he used them to support what his prejudice (he would have said his insight or cast of mind) secretly favored. He started with definite assumptions, and his selection of probabilities was made on the basis of whether or not they tended to support his assumption.

Froude's two positive rules of thought divorced him completely from Newman's mode of thinking. Holding absolute certainty to be, humanly speaking, impossible, he deprecated any attempts to delude oneself, by sheer force of will, into a state of security. He held that doubts were sacred, since only by the vitalizing force of this residuum of doubt could the mind keep alive to the possibility of error. So was the search for truth literally unceasing.

Froude was by far the more individualistic in his philosophy; he believed that self-reliance was pleasing to God, and that honest error was more moral than willing oneself to believe what was repugnant to rationality. Newman, on the other hand, had a natural disposition for the Catholic manner of thought. Feeling obedience to be a cardinal virtue, he followed unquestioningly the promptings of his conscience. He relied not so much upon himself as upon God. His was not the heroic spirit which fought on alone to whatever was the end; he sought always for support and trusted where he could not see.

In his letter Froude made only one concession to Newman's point of view, and that was on the important matter of insight. "I do not overlook the view," he says above, "that 'spiritual insight is granted as the reward of Faith,' nor do I venture to judge that (in some shape) it is an impossible or even an improbable one." He then qualified his statement to exclude the purely theological definition of faith. In admitting the possibility and even the probability of insight, that is, of a power of mind enabling one to see beyond the measure of ordinary men, Froude left free from criticism that point which later became the very core of Newman's philosophical treatise. Beginning with insight Newman elaborated his theory of the illative sense, a psychological quality of the mind which, by a natural but complicated process, unerringly recognized supernatural truths. The illative sense then was Newman's means of reconciling what Froude had said was the "source of disagreement between us . . . . seated in the very principle of thinking and of concluding."

No one would venture to claim that Froude was alone responsible for the argument as Newman finally developed it; the influences upon him were innumerable, but it is of some significance to note that Newman did rely most heavily upon the one point to which Froude felt he could least object, and it is perhaps of yet more significance that Newman, in his reply, said that he would keep the "letter before me to use."

Jan. 2, 1860.

My dear Wm,

Your letter of this morning has been a very great comfort to me. The greatest of evils in the intercourse of friends is the ignorance about each others feelings, not by your fault for you wrote to me at Rome, not by mine, because I did not get your letter, nor by my fault several years afterwards, when I did get it, though at the moment I don't recollect enough to explain. I have not known where you were, and whatever I have said has been doubtless as you say, in opposite, because I have been striking out with the dark.

And now that I know clearly where to find you, I don't suppose that I am going to argue, or indeed can.

The line you draw out in your letter is familiar to me and I don't even know when I began to feel it, not that you do not bring it out more clearly than I perhaps have done to myself. I shall keep your letter before me to use. Still I have long meditated on its subject. I think it a fallacy—but I don't think it easy to show it to be so. It is one of various points which I have steadily set before me as requiring an answer, and an answer from me. I indirectly refer to it in the Preface to my "Anglicanism."

I am habitually praying God to direct me whether to take up the line of subjects on which it lies or to devote my remaining years to some other undertaking. At this very time friends have been saying masses for me with this very intention.

I am saying all this to show how little I can mean to be disrespectful to your view of the subject and how little I should dream of putting it down in a few magisterial words, at the same time I do with all my heart, and what is more to the purpose, with all my reason think it a sophism, (but you will perfectly understand) a sophism may require an effort of almost genius to overset with its logical and luminous solution. In truth I think there is a far deeper philosophy on the subject than yours, if I could develop it, much lies in the meaning of the words certainty and doubt, much again in our duties to a *person*, as e. g. a friend. Religion is not merely a science but a *devotion;* but though I have thought much upon the subject, I have written nothing which so satisfied me as to make me think of publication. I don't think it practically bears upon Hurrell's [6] case but I am relying on his professions or promises of perseverance which he has made to me. Of course he intends to persevere and ought to intend, else he ought not to take so solemn a step. He ought not to be playing at religion. I think he would persevere, because I think he really at present believes that God speaks to him through the Church. I know a man may lose faith, but it is very difficult. I meant that what influenced Hurrell was faith, not a fancy. On the other hand, I think he could no more promise that he *would* examine in the future than he could decently, becomingly or dutifully promise that his mind should ever be open to evidence that his parents were imposters and hypocrites.

Forgive me if there was anything rude in my last paragraph. I spoke as I did in order to bring out the position of my mind toward you.

When I became a Catholic, I think I wrote to Rogers to beg his forgiveness if in anything I had acted unkindly toward him. My severance from him and others is a wound which will never heal. This is no inconsistency to say so, though I feel myself in possession of supernatural truth and consolation. The natural heart has wounds as well as the body.

Yours most affy,

J. H. N.

Newman's indelicate reference to " imposters and hypocrites " was a harsh remark such as he seldom permitted himself in intercourse with friends, but his making it and at the same time apologizing for it shows how different was the temper of his mind from Froude's. To Newman's way of thinking it would be undutiful for a son to entertain evidence of a derogatory nature concerning his father. He considered emotional and conventional factors, and to him it seemed only

---

[6] Froude's son.

right that in such a case unfavorable evidence ought to be excluded by an act of the will from consideration. With him such things were " not done "; it outraged his sense of decorum and gentlemanly conduct. Nothing could be further from Froude's viewpoint. To him it seemed an immoral use of the faculties to allow prejudices, whether of filial love or of duty, to interfere with the reception and proper evaluation of evidence, no matter to what conclusion that evidence pointed. This small matter serves as an admirable practical illustration of the different intellectual constitution of the two men.

Froude appreciated fully how different was the cast of Newman's mind from his own, and for this very reason he was particularly interested in what Newman had to say. This feeling was shared by large numbers of Oxford men, many of whom had heard Newman's sermons and knew him as a serious if conservative thinker. Even those least likely to agree with him on philosophical grounds could but be charmed by the flow of his words and the brilliance of his dialectic. It was, then, largely because Newman occupied so extraordinary a position in English thought that Froude urgently pressed him to do what he felt no other man could do so well; that was, to set down clearly and at length the concatenation of the argument for belief.

My dear Newman, 15 Jan. 1860

I most heartily wish, (and I have heard others who think much as I do express the same wish with equal heartiness) that you would really and fully work out this question—it is indeed one which you more than anybody else have been felt by those who know you, to be competent to examine.

But in the meantime I want you to tell me whether when you say that you feel the view which I endeavoured to express is a sophism, you meant that it is so in reference to the pursuit of truth generally or only in reference to the pursuit of Religious Truth.

What you say about religion being of a nature of "a duty to a person" bears on this point. And I remember to have been long ago much struck with a passage of yours (in Anglican difficulties I think) very like that (last but one) paragraph in your letter, which you in the succeeding sentence of it referred to as perhaps needing apology—I mean keeping the mind open to evidence of one's friends faults—these passages also bear on the subject—and with so much force that I am far indeed from feeling that the most personally pointed expression of the view they contain is out of place or needs apology. Without attempting to generalize, or to recite the ins and outs of thought through which the passage I have referred to, long ago led me, I will only say that I came ultimately to and rested in that very proposition about my children's duties toward myself, which you felt pained at having barely suggested. So long as my children think of me fairly—and weigh evidence about me fairly—and do not go out of their depth in inquiry—so long as they take in conducting that particular enquiry all the care which the pursuit of truth (the honest pursuit of it) requires of the pursuer everywhere—I see no reason to complain of their being ready to receive evidence that I am an imposter and a hypocrite. If I am such, I desire that they should know it—or if I flinch from thus saying here, it is only as I flinch from it while my better sense tells me I ought not to flinch. But I feel I have a right to require of them that they should not select the evidence which is *against* me—that they must not be suspicious, Othello's fault was not that he judged her passionately, [but] to him being "jealous," "trifles light as air" were "confirmation strong as Holy Writ."

One might say much more on this subject, but I believe I have said enough to indicate what I wanted to express, and probably I should not make it clearer by enlarging on it.

Believe me, sir, yours affectionately,
W. Froude.

Newman could but be dismayed at the giant's task to which Froude was setting him. Far from being trifles light as air, the questions were of such a nature that probably no answer generally acceptable could be given to them. In replying, however, Newman did expose the kernel of his thought so far as it had matured by 1860 and at the same time begged leave to submit further points for critical analysis and judgment.

Jan. 18, 1860.

My dear Wm,

It is a cause of great sadness to me, when I look back at my life, to consider how my time has been frittered away, and how much I might have done had I pursued one subject. Had not each year brought its own duties, I should have turned to the subject which I spoke of long ago but it is not one to be taken up by halves, and now, how many years have I?

As to your question whether, when I say that I feel the view of the subject which you put out a sophism, I mean that it is so in reference to the pursuit of Truth, generally, or only in reference to the pursuit of "religious truth." Speaking under the correction of my fuller thought I should say

(1) that I not only do not mean that there is anything sophistical in the principles on which non-religious truth is pursued at present, but that theologians (who ought to know in Arte sua) all affirm that Christianity is proved by the same rigorous scientific processes by which it is proved that we have an Indian Empire or that the earth goes around the sun. I mean the proof is in this same line or order, for of course it is difficult to say whether we have more or less right, or neither more nor less to be certain that India belongs to the English (Empire) than that the earth goes around the sun.

(2) But the scientific proof of Christianity is not the popular, practical, personal evidence on which a given individual believes in it. And here I think it is where your question really comes in. I should differ from you, if I understand you, in thinking that there is a popular and personal way of arriv-

ing at certainty in Christianity as logical as that which is arrived at by scientific methods in subjects non-religious. I was struck how table turning was put down—by the sort of argument indeed which I originally heard you used in conversation—in the world at large in a few days by the authority of a great name, Faraday, presenting to the public one argument which was received on its plausibility by the man, or on his word without trial.

I consider the proof (grounds) on which a given individual believes in Christianity are of this character or order. But they are so far more cogent as to lead legitimately not only to opinion or passive acceptance but to certainty as cogent as scientific proof. Nay I go further, I think that [there] is a sophism in (considering) the certainty of secular science so far superior to the certainty, or persuasion as you would call it, of the personal evidence for Christianity. I suspect that when all scientific proof, even for the existence of India, is examined microscopically there will be found hiatus[es] in the logical sequence so considerable as to lend to the question " are there no broad, just principles of knowledge which will protect us from scepticism in all reasoning about things external to us, both scientific and popular?" As to what you say about a person, I don't think we should disagree in principle when the subject was fully worked out.

I have heavy trials and discouragements in the midst of enormous mercies, but should I be led to pursue the subject of this letter (which would be by very slow marches) I should ask your leave to put various points before you, as iron girders are sent to the trying house.

I have a husky cough which makes me almost anxious, as being something new, and so resolved not to go.

Ever yours affy

J. H. N.

Newman's reply clearly displays his cleavage from Froude's belief. He affirms that, although such will not be his own method, Christianity may be proved by valid logical reasoning along scientific lines and that theologians all maintain this. His reason for believing in such a possibility is that ultimately secular and religious arguments rest upon assumptions; that is, actually there is a hiatus in the rigorous scientific proof of anything whatsoever (which may be generally admitted), and since every proof is built finally upon an assumption, the structure reared upon a religious assumption need not for that reason alone be more unstable than one set upon a secular or scientific assumption. In so viewing the problem Newman disregarded the important question of degree. Froude readily recognized the ultimate hiatus in scientific proof, but he maintained that such a hiatus was infinitesimal compared to the hiatus to be encountered in attempting the scientific proof of a religious question. Newman of course recognized that there was a difference in the hiatuses, but to him the question of degree was irrelevant. And it is only logical that it should have been, for he had always refused steadfastly to weigh evidence and to give assent to a particular proposition simply because it was by quantitative measure more probable than another. For him, ten or ten thousand difficulties did not necessarily make one doubt, whereas for Froude to have reached any conclusion over so many difficulties would have been nearly impossible.

However, it was by no means upon rigorous scientific principles, as Froude was accustomed to use them, that Newman proposed to build his argument for belief. Newman did not believe that it was by strictly scientific means that a " given individual " arrived at certainty of religious belief. He chose to make his proof in another manner which he claimed to be nevertheless as logical and as valid as a strictly scientific proof. He proposed to examine the " popular, practical, personal evidence on which a given individual believes " in Christianity, and to show that the resulting certainty was " as cogent as scientific proof." In his argument the validity of " personal evidence " was all important, and under the head of personal evidence came conscience, " inner feelings," prejudices, desires to believe, in fact almost everything that would seem to a scientist most in need of exclusion. To these arguments he would add also the very Catholic one of authority, which in this case would largely rest upon revelation. He expected Froude to admit the overwhelming weight authority would add to his argument, just as on the occasion of a well known investigation into table rapping, authority, in the name of Faraday, had demolished the opposition of a group of men not themselves scientists.

Newman's proposal was, in short, to establish religious certainty not by scientific means (though that would be possible) but by other means " just as good." The question still remains whether or not the means, which are certainly not scientific, are in fact " just as good "—so far as Froude was concerned, they never were.

Froude, in the letter which follows, has pointed out the weak points in Newman's argument in a fashion so incisive and so clear as to make any additional comment supererogatory.

Elmsleigh-Paignton
Torquay,
25 Jan 1860

My dear Newman,

It seems strange to connect your history with the idea of your having frittered away your time, even though the idea be started by yourself.

For myself when I ask myself the question (as I have had to do) " how can I venture to think that I should be one of those to find out truly the safety in a position which men so wise and good continue to think fatally dangerous," I say in reply " it was the four lepers who sat in the gate, afraid to take part in the trials of their fellow citizens, and ready to fall away to the Syrians for the bare chance of a meal, who discovered the siege was raised."

I have already said that I do not venture to enter into controversy with you, but yet there are one or two things which your letter impels me to try to say in reference to it.

Putting out of consideration for a moment the personal certainty arrived at without scientific proof, it seems to me that you attribute to scientific proof a cogency and completeness of conviction, which in the domain of " science " technically so called, none of the higher minds which occupy that domain, attribute to such proofs. I have seen either in your letters or in something which you have published, more than one illustrative reference to the Newtonian system, as if it were to be treated (or as if at least " science " treated it) as being established beyond the possibility of confutation or of change—and in your last note, you refer to the proof of the earth going round the sun as an illustration of the *sort of* proof by which Christianity is proved. It is of course difficult to understand exactly how strong or complete meaning another person attaches to the word " certainty," but there is a test which seems to me effective as showing the limitation of its meaning which the best men of science adopt. They would all emphatically disclaim such a certainty as would justify them in saying (whether [of] the Newtonian theory, or of any other positive however *quasi fundamental*) " I always *will* hold to this—I *will* earnestly *endeavour* to combat arguments brought against it and will resist the inclination to be swayed by them "—They would be as anxious to eliminate from their confidence, the disposition to say this as an Iron Master is to get rid of sulphur and of phosphorous from the produce of his furnace. It seems to me that the tendency to say "*I will*" in reference to belief is the characteristic not of scientific but of personal proof.

There are, no doubt, very many practically able men of science, who, not less than other man, are overflowing with the personal element of certainty, and who talk of the "unfailing certainty" of their processes in consequence. For the "Personal certainty" is, I think, never so confident as when it seems to itself to have a scientific basis to rest on—like Micah when he said he had a Levite to his Priest.

What is really the mental nature of the process which produces what you call personal certainty I do not at all know or think I know—I believe however that I know as a fact the state of mind which you indicate, both in myself and others, though it is very possible I may be mistaken in saying so, or that I confuse under that one term, states of mind between which you would discriminate. So far, however, as I understand you rightly, I do admit that I think scientific proof, or certainty derived from it, far more certain than the Personal certainty—not however because I think the former so very certain, but because the latter seems to me so very doubtful. And I think the latter admits its inferiority by always trying to fall back on "a reason," (I mean a real conclusive reason, such reason as scientific proof deals with) when questioned or controverted. Viewed in the abstract, its claims seem to rest on its being of the nature of an insight—but yet to take the illustration sketched by you in the preface to "Romanism," when you describe a party struggling in the dark over a pathless moor, if those of the party who said they could *see* their way were, when questioned about it, to fall back on the same kind of intimations by which the rest were *feeling* their ways, a brush here and a stone there, the direction of the wind, etc, etc, and were found to stumble on after the rest, and as often to be obliged to retrace their steps,—the others would be right in taking this as a mark that their consciousness of "sight" was a delusion.

For I suppose *you* would admit that multitudes of those who *experience the sensation* of personal conviction are nevertheless in error. I mean they often turn out to have been in

WILLIAM FROUDE

error in reference to questions where their conclusions on views are ultimately confronted with and confuted by the experience of the end. But I am going beyond the limit I had proposed to myself—and I will only now refer to the "table turning" question; not in its relation to the question of certainty, but in reference to the mode in which Faraday treated it. This, it seems to me, was different from what you suppose. For I think his authority did little for him but to get him a hearing—everybody knew that he entirely discredited the facts and the theory, but they did not the less adhere to what seemed to be the facts. Faraday did not bring evidence against the facts, or properly speaking, argue against the theories—he only contrived a very simple experiment, which he induced several of the most enthusiastic table turners to try, which experiment showed them that the facts they thought they saw were not the real facts—that their own unaided senses had misled them and that in part they had deceived themselves, that when they thought or persuaded themselves they were not pushing the table, they were in fact pushing it; and that when by a simple contrivance he enabled them to see whether they were pushing or were not pushing, and in what direction, they no longer did push and the table no longer moved, so much for the *facts* of the table turning experiments—. As regards the theories which people had made up about them, trying to connect them with unknown phenomena and laws of electricity etc. he showed first that plainly those who made up these theories, knew nothing at least of the laws of electricity etc. as they were understood by the best men of the day. He did, however, so far argue on the case, as to point, very slightly yet very clearly, a few of the mechanical contradictions (measured by the ordinary law of mechanics) which would follow from or were involved in the alleged facts and theories, but he did this not as a regular controversial answer, but rather to make men ashamed who had theorized so confidently, without *once perceiving* how immediately their theories came into contact with the simplest forms of the best established laws, it was not that these latter were infallible, but that the former had not decently established a claim to a hearing.

I think it was not Faraday's authority, but the natural collapse of a delusion when thus confronted, which put down table turning, it was not that people were convinced that they were wrong, but that they saw when helped to look fairly, that they had no decent reason for supposing themselves right.

This table turning matter induced Faraday to put out a little tract or pamphlet on mental education—I wonder whether you saw it, it contained a dictum which seemed to help me very much to consolidate my floating notions. He said that when a young man, he had been discussing some question with Dr. Wollaston who, in support of his own view, said, half sportively, " I will bet you three to one it is so and so "—Faraday said he had sneered at the phrase in reference to scientific pursuit of Truth, when Dr. W. replied very gravely, that he had intended in that way to express his measure of *preponderance* of the evidence in favor of the view he adopted. This had been to him (Faraday) a great saying ever after, and his own dictum in reference to it was that " the force of certainty of our conclusions ought to be proportioned to the force of the evidence by which they are supported." And thus he himself, though one of the greatest discoverers and profoundest thinkers on scientific questions of the present day, is also perhaps the most diffident in all his views. What I have written will I fear, seem in many ways beside the mark.

Ever yours affectionately,
W. Froude.

For the difficulties Froude showed to be inherent in the argument, Newman had at the time no further solution, and he hesitated even to contemplate the onerous task of attacking them. Newman was then in his darkest years; fifty-nine years old, his life seemed nearly finished. Days full of rewarding toil, like those spent at Oxford, had quite passed away. The battles were now being fought by younger men, and it seemed unlikely that veterans would be called into active service. Newman's mind, like many another of great depth, made haste slowly in pushing back some little way the limits of human speculation. It was not until four years later that, searching deep in the recesses of his mind, he began to find the answers to the questions Froude propounded. For the moment he had perforce to content himself with seeming inactivity.

V

CORRESPONDENCE THROUGH AUGUST, 1864

V

CORRESPONDENCE THROUGH AUGUST, 1864

DIFFICULTIES of a practical sort succeeded the spiritual ones Froude experienced upon Hurrell's conversion. The most pressing of these was how best to proceed in the matter of completing his son's education. Under the existing conditions it was nearly impossible for a Roman Catholic to gain admittance to any of the better colleges at Oxford, and consequently it seemed that Hurrell would be largely cut off from the benefits and pleasures of a normal university career. Instead of entering one of the colleges at Oxford Hurrell took up private residence there in the family of William Fishburn Donkin, the Savilian Professor of Astronomy. Froude was bitterly disappointed at the necessity for such a course, which seems first to have been suggested by Newman, but he agreed to it as the best thing possible at the time. Even in this partial seclusion there was real danger that Hurrell's religion would still set him apart from his fellow students. Newman offered his best advice as one who in any Oxford matters knew whereof he spoke. His summary of the situation in a letter to Mrs. Froude is rather more worldly than was usually the case with him.

> The Oratory, Birmingham
> December 29th, 1859.[1]

Hurrel went off this morning before your letter came . . . . I had already intended to write to you about his future, as you are the natural medium on the subject between William and me. I mean William may *wish* to know my opinion.

What makes me think so is that Hurrell has shown me letters of Mr. Donkin's to his father, so very carefully worded

[1] Ward, *Life*, I, 646-47.

that I can't help thinking that I am intended to see them. And I will tell you just what I think about them.

I wish him to continue at Oxford and to go up for honours in mathematics—this is his father's plan, and an excellent one. Donkin proposes his being entered at New Inn Hall and *residing in lodgings*. It seems to me desirable he should be entered somewhere—else, he can't go for honours—but I don't relish the lodging plan.

1. It makes him *dependent* on New Inn Hall for his status —and New Inn Hall has always been a ridiculous place—used to be called Botany Bay—and now has no men at all belonging to it, (nor had it when I first went to Oxford).

2. Having no society *there,* he is thrown upon the odds and ends of Oxford residents, and, even if he does not make third rate acquaintances, is at least out of the Oxford world.

3. There can't be a place more full of temptation to him, than to be without any discipline in lodgings.

4. And how forlorn is he to have his dinners in from a pastry-cook, and how expensive!

What I hope is, judging from the present state of things, that Donkin will continue him on.

Donkin himself seems to have no objection, (unless he had another undergraduate lodger), but to fear that Hurrell will be aggressive—i. e. will not let the inmates of the house alone. I don't say this is unreasonable, but I think it will prove an unfounded apprehension.

I mean, Hurrell's business is not to talk of his religion, not to argue, not to attempt to proselytize, but to attend to himself and to mind his studies. Religious controversy is an edged tool—he might find it far easier to unsettle another, to make him restless and discontented, nay to inspire him with a spirit of criticism and scepticism, than to make a good Catholic. See what happened the other day. I am told that the young Catholic at Lincoln College converted (as it is called) some University (College) friend. The father and mother come up and persuade him back again, so he is received, baptized, absolved, all for nothing but the scandal.

I don't think then that Donkin ought to have any ground

of complaint or fear as regards Hurrell. H. ought to keep to his religious duties, and fag hard—see those acquaintances which come in his way—take an interest in what goes on—and keep his religion to himself. He has a great deal to learn; and, though he must not deny his religion, he must not obtrude it. The Donkins seem most desirable people. I don't think they will wish to molest him, and he must not molest them.

If at Donkin's he could come up here from time to time for the Sunday. I don't suppose Donkin would object,—and this would be a very great point. He will require a great deal of looking after at first,—for at present he depends on others and asks what he is to do. I do not think he would be happy unless he had some one to consult.

A month had not passed before Newman's fears were realized. There arose the question of family prayers at which the Donkins expected Hurrell's attendance, but by Catholic rule he was forbidden to attend the worship of those external to the Church. Newman did his best to smooth the matter over, but there appeared to be no other egress from the awkward situation except the rather trimming one he suggested in writing to Froude:

The Oratory B^m.
Jan. 31, 1860.

My dear William,

I fully enter into the difficulty of the Family Prayers—and I had the greatest desire to give way upon it. Not satisfied with my own judgment, I consulted a friend; but we agreed together that I must say what I said.

When I say " my own judgment," I do not mean that I have been able to use my own private discretion, or to have an opinion *strictly* my own. I will say how the case stands.

From time immemorial, from the earliest ages, members of the church have been forbidden " communicatio in sacris " with those who were external to it. This prohibition is not intended as the expression of any judgment on this or that individual, but is a general and formal decision upon the position of non-catholics as *such*.

The sole question then is about the fact, the application of the principle, viz. *what is* communicatio in sacris? On this point there has been a difference of opinion, and in various times, places, dioceses and communities it has been answered variously.

That it used in England to be answered *in favour* of such Family Prayers, as are in question, I know well. It may by some be so answered still, for what I know; as by the Jesuits, though I doubt it much. I should be very glad, if Hurrell could get it answered in his favour; and he would have quite a right to avail himself of the permission, if he could get it from any quarter. In a matter of practice, there are of the two opinions current, a more lax and a more rigorous.

But for myself, I must go by the traditions and rules, in which I find myself. I may perhaps be in possession of information concerning what those who have a claim on my obedience wish, so as to make it impossible for me to give any decision but one. And I really in my conscience do think that I have interpreted the communicatio in sacris, as the Church means me to interpret it. I really think she does not allow me in this matter to judge for myself as to what is the meaning of the words. But, while I say this, I have no right to force my own conclusion on another; and if there be others who take a different view, and think such Family Prayers are not a communicatio in sacris (which I much doubt) they have as much right to their opinion as I to mine.

There is only one concession I could make, which seems so nugatory and disrespectful, that I don't like to make it; but, as another may think differently, I will mention it:—Hurrell might attend Family Prayers, provided he took a crucifix or Garden of the Soul in his hand, and said his own prayers to himself during the devotions. This is practised in the case of servants.

Ever yours aff[ly]
John H. Newman.[2]

P. S. You may show this letter to any one.

---

[2] Part of this letter is given in Ward, *Life,* I, 647.

Such a course was adopted, and Hurrell, carrying a crucifix, attended the Family Prayers with full mental reservation. Of this the Donkins were at first unaware, and their subsequent discovery of so much "Roman guile" was too much for them—or at least, as Newman suggests, for Mrs. Donkin—and Hurrell's attendance at Prayers ceased abruptly. Newman's comment to Froude was characteristically frank:

> The Oratory
> Birmingham
> March 24, 1860.
>
> My dear William,
>
> ... As to Donkin, I assure you I quite estimate his forbearance, and think I should have acted at least as strongly as he in his position. He and his wife, I have always felt a great respect for—and should before now have sent them some sort of civil message, except that from something Hurrell dropped when he was here, I thought it would not be well received.
>
> I had been ungallant enough, on thinking over the matter, to impute the difficulty which had arisen to her, not to him—but really not in any unkind spirit, for I think it must be very irritating to a lady to have a boy in the house who reminds her twice a day that he is of a different religion from hers—nor does it at all tell against her in a religious point of view in my judgment, but just the reverse.
>
> I don't think there is any inconsistency in my saying all this, being what I am, but I never have been in the practice of measuring my words with such as you, my dear William, and I feel just what I have said, and therefore say it.
>
> Ever yours affect[ly]
> John H. Newman.
>
> P. S. I shall be more at leisure to see Hurrell after Easter, than I should have been now.

Similar unpleasantnesses frequently occurred, and

Hurrell's life, externally, was not made more happy by reason of his intellectual beliefs. What Hurrell was just coming to realize, Newman had of course long known from personal experience. Concerning the boy's situation Newman wrote Mrs. Froude:

> It is bringing out the fact that a Catholic cannot comfortably or profitably go to Oxford. Oxford belongs to the country and country's religion—and I very much doubt if Cambridge would have been better; we see the bad consequences of what we decide on, whatever it may be and have no experience of such other steps, as we do *not* take.
>
> Again, we must not disguise from ourselves that this trial will in a measure follow him through life, his being a Catholic will stand in the way of his forming friendships and getting on in his profession, whatever it is. But it will not improve matters at the moment to tell him so.

Hurrell had no sooner become a Catholic than Mrs. Froude began delicately to urge Edmund also to confess that faith. Edmund listened to her the more readily because, by reason of his youth (he was but fifteen), he was unable as yet to appreciate his father's side of the argument. What weighed most with his immaturity was quite naturally the emotional persuasion of his mother—and the romantic appeal of Newman, writing, teaching, praying in the secluded Oratory at Edgbaston. Within two years of his brother's conversion he was himself ready to become a Catholic. From school he wrote long letters to his mother concerning his state of mind, and she passed them on not to her husband but to Newman as the person most fitting to see them.

The O^y B^m
Nov. 13/62.

My dear Mrs Froude,

Eddy's letter, which I return herewith, is a wonderful one.

WILLIAM FROUDE 149

A boy who can write such a letter may well be left to fight his own battles—and had better be. Your advice to him is quite right. He ought to write to Wm with as little delay as possible—and he will naturally let him know that he has kept his feelings so much to himself, that you are surprised yourself to read what he says, tho' you may have hoped how things were going. Thank you very much for writing to me—please God, I will say Mass for your intention about him. Since you now know, Wm should know too, certainly, as you say. . . .

When on April 9, 1863, Newman received Edmund into the Catholic Church, he at once announced the fact to Froude in a letter particularly painful in that it struck again at those intellectual principles almost as dear to Froude as his son's spiritual welfare. Appreciating as he did fully Froude's point of view, Newman did not find it easy to describe his own part in Edmund's reception. He set down his feelings of the moment in a letter which, when he came to send it, he revised considerably. The following is a full text of Newman's rough draft as he kept it by him.[8]

My dear William,

I have received Eddy into the Catholic Church today. He satisfied me that for some months you had been aware of his intention of being received at this time. If he was to be received, I felt you would rather that I received him, than that another should do so.

I don't write this with any wish or intention of troubling you to send me an answer (for it would only increase the pain) but will you let me, as a relief to myself, explain my feelings on one or two points to you.

1. It stands to reason I cannot argue as I should argue if I were in your position. In that case I might say to him,

---

[8] The somewhat shorter letter actually sent to Froude is given in Ward, *Life,* I, 649-50. The portions in parentheses are corrections in style. This draft is at Edgbaston.

"wait till your judgment is more mature"—but, as it is, while on the one hand I (have every reason to) believe that he is acting deliberately and religiously, on right motives and on rational grounds, and on the other I believe him to have come to a right conclusion, to be embracing what I myself am firmly persuaded is the truth, and what he might not be granted from above another opportunity of embracing, if he did not embrace it now.

2. Nor do I feel, as I should perhaps, if I were you, that he is putting himself under a sort of intellectual tyranny by making an act which he is not allowed to reverse. I say this because I do not think the prohibition on the part of the Church to her children to doubt and imagine (enquire into her claims and teachings) is so much a practical rule as a scientific principle, laid down to make the theological system logically consistent with itself. A man is kept from skepticism, not by any external prohibition, but by admiration, trust, and love. While he admires trusts and loves our Lord and his Church, those feelings prohibit him from doubt, *they* guard and protect his faith—the real prohibition is from within. But suppose they go—suppose he ceases to have admiration, trust, love of our Lord and His Church—(well, I will not deny that it is nothing, even that dead, unfruitful, un-saving faith which remains,) because it keeps him in an external position in which it is easier and more likely for his former feelings and convictions to return, than if he openly committed himself to some other profession: but as to his state substantially, how is it better than if he went on to allow himself to doubt? he would indeed, in my view of the matter, sin further, but he is already a dead branch and an actual present incumbrance to the Catholic community. And moreover, in the state in which he is in that case, the external prohibition will not (probably) suffice to keep him from doubting. And thus it avails in neither case. While he loves and trusts it is not needed (needless): and when he does not love and trust, it will not act (is impotent).

Of course I both trust and expect that Eddy will continue in firm faith in our Lord and his Church: but my feeling is grounded on the confidence that the more he experiences what the Catholic religion is, its support, its comfort, its peace, and its depth, the greater devotion will he have towards it as the gift of the one living and true God to his creatures and the greater repugnance he will feel to put it on its trial, as if he then had heard of it for the first time. To bid him authoritatively not to doubt, will be as irrelevant, as to bid him not to maim himself or put out his eyes. But I say all this merely to explain with what a view of the matter I have made him a Catholic: not at all expecting you even to acknowledge the receipt of this letter, unless you actually wish to do so.

Immediately after his conversion, Edmund left Bradfield to enter the Oratory School to complete his education under a mind among the most considerable—and the most misunderstood—in England. Newman's letter to Mrs. Froude after Edmund's conversion was typically a mixture of high rejoicing, of devout hopes, and of the most trivial details.

The Oratory B^m
April 19, 1863.

My dear Mrs Froude,

Eddy was the best letter I could send you, so I did not think it necessary to write. But my *reason* for not writing was, that, when it came to the point, dear William weighed on my mind, and it seemed unkind to be rejoicing with you at news which would so distress him. I wrote to him by the first post, telling him I did not expect an answer.

Eddy seemed well inclined to come here. I hope he will. But William must authorize it. You say he has—but I am very unwilling that it should take place without his direct assent. How is this to be? If he gives it to *you*, it will be quite enough for me.

Another thing—the terms—our ordinary terms are 80 guineas a year. I don't know what they are at Bradfield—but if Eddy were to be one of the Woolwich class, as we wish (but that is another matter) the terms will be much higher. Mr Ward, on inquiry, found that, if he placed his son with a Woolwich grinder, he would have to pay £160 a year; and so he gives us, on our undertaking the work ourselves, and getting Mr O'Hagar for the purpose, that sum. However, you may be sure, we shall not make any point of the Terms, if those I have mentioned seem excessive. We should give Eddy one of the rooms in our house, if he preferred it to sleeping in the school houses.

I have said nothing of Eddy himself—and I have nothing to say but what you would like to hear me say, and what you must know far better than I, who have seen him for the first, and for so short a time. He is most single-minded and straightforward, and, as thoughtful and clever as he is good. God grant he may ever remain as he is—and that he may lose nothing of what he has, while he gains a great deal more.

Love and congratulations to all of you—and best Easter greetings. I wrote to Hurrell the other day.

> Ever yours aff^{ly}
> John H. Newman.

Newman throughout his life continued to hope that some day it might be granted to him also to receive William into the Catholic Church, and more poignantly than ever did he cherish this hope at the time when he was receiving Edmund. In concluding a letter to Sister Mary Gabriel, April 7, 1863, Newman said:

... I am engaged just now in receiving one of the Froudes—a boy of sixteen who arrived here yesterday from School. My dear friend, his father, who is not a Catholic has seen his children one after another, (this is the fourth) received into the Church; and he has borne it so gently, so meekly, so tenderly, (though it has given him a sense of desolation more cruel to bear) that I do trust God's mercy has the same gift in store for himself. Please give him your prayers, and ask your Sisters to do the like. It is the infallibility of the Church which is his stumbling stone. He would confess that her authority is probable, but he cannot receive her absolute infallibility, and since she claims (as he thinks) what she has not, therefore the claim itself is a proof against her. What a good Catholic he would make, if the grace of God touched his heart. Get our Lady to ask for him—what a joyful day it would be!

>Ever yrs affect^ly in Christ
>John H. Newman
>of the Oratory.

For both Newman and Froude the following year of 1864 was one of great distress. Newman with unimaginable pain forced himself to lay bare in a public controversy the history of his intimate thoughts. Froude suffered none the less because his were trials in which the world could have little interest. His little daughter, Mary, became dangerously ill early in the spring, and with the ebbing of her life went too her father's last spiritual consolation. Too young to comprehend the fierce disputes of religious persuasion, Mary had remained a Protestant, loving her father more than the life she was to relinquish. On the last evening in May the child burst a blood vessel in her lung. With all the family about her bed, Froude took her in his arms and " asked her if she would like the clergyman as the illness was taking a bad turn." " Oh—directly? " she replied, unaware that anything could quite loose those arms about her. Gently he told her, " I don't know whether the danger is immediate; Mr. Pridham will tell us. It won't frighten you, will it, my darling? " " No," she replied. " I thought it was so when the blood came. I'm sorry." And presently she added,

"Pray don't think I'm unhappy about it; for I think I'd rather. But I'm sorry for Papa."[4]

For Froude there was nobody to whom he could speak in full understanding of his loss. Mrs. Froude had the especial sympathy of Newman on which to rely. On the day of her daughter's funeral she wrote:

> . . . now that they have carried my darling child to Denbury, I am left alone in the house, and I feel that nothing could relieve me so much as writing to you. All Monday he was very much overwhelmed; that last terrible half hour, during which he held her in his arms, was always present to his imagination.[5]

Two months had not passed before Froude suffered another blow, in some ways the greatest of his life. This was the knowledge that Edmund proposed to abandon science to enter the priesthood. Froude had so far borne with patience the loss of his family to the Catholic Church, but he had had no expectation that any of them would make a vocation of religious life. Moreover, he felt that Edmund, who was but sixteen, was far too young to make so important a decision, and yet he feared that were he to prevent him from following his desire, Edmund might relinquish his interest in science without finding a substitute. Edmund's proposal had been made without much forethought, for he had apparently arrived at the decision after a retreat in which a visiting priest, Father Suffield, seems first to have suggested the idea. Even Newman, in whose charge Edmund had been placed at the Oratory, was largely unaware of the direction of his thoughts until Edmund made known his intention as a settled thing.

[4] Edmund Froude's account as written to Newman.
[5] June 4, 1864.

Newman, as he had always done, wrote the news to Froude with no attempt at palliation.

> Paddington Hotel,
> July 19, 1864.
>
> My dear William,
>
> I must collect my thoughts to write to you. I am here for a day or two having had a talk with Eddie before I left.
>
> I told him that *he* must speak to you on the subject which he opened to me, and that then I would write. It seemed to me better, and so it was settled—but, since leaving him, I came to think I had better write first. He talks of returning home tomorrow: and you may like to be prepared.
>
> He told me that Fr Suffield told him that he had a vocation for the Priesthood. Before his retreat, I had warned him against acting under excitement. He said yesterday, as if in answer to this, that nothing that had passed in the retreat had moved him, but that for some time he has wished to ask the question, and that he should have asked me, if he had not had the opportunity of asking Fr Suffield.
>
> I said to him that it would never surprise me to find that he had a true call to be a Priest, but that I did not think he could be sure of it yet. He wished to stay in the Oratory some little time—I suppose Fr Suffield had recommended it—but it seemed to me his better course was to see you at once.
>
> I think it exceedingly likely that he will ultimately find such a great desire and such a feeling of duty to give himself to the direct service of God, as to make it almost clear that it will end in his entering the ecclesiastical state—but I certainly could not myself recommend him to make up his mind at once. Then he says that you will have had all the expense of sending him to Oxford for nothing.
>
> I have much anxiety lest this should be an additional pain to you. Yet I do not know what to say more than I have said. His primary duty is to obey you—I do not see that he can plead any sense of ecclesiastical duty strong enough to overcome this—yet, just as I think he will go through Oxford (if

sent there) as a religious youth keeping his principles, so I expect that he will keep to this wish.

I think you had better tell him that I have changed my mind and written to you at once.

Ever yours aff^{ly}
John H. Newman.

The news struck too deeply for Froude to do more than acknowledge Newman's letter.

Elmsleigh,
20th July, 1864

My dear Newman,

You could not have written more kindly. But what you tell me is a great blow to me, one of the blows which make me wish at the moment that what is to be done be done quickly.

In one side of Eddy's mind there was growing up a fund of common feeling and interest with me, and this seemed to give one little spot of light, but this intention quenches it by what seems to me (though I can well understand how it will seem widely otherwise to others) not an impulse really divine and from above.

But it is useless giving vent to what on my part is hasty and impulsive feelings.

Ever yours affectionately,
W. Froude.

Neither Mrs. Froude nor Newman was convinced that Edmund had a call sufficiently authoritative to warrent his deserting science in which he was becoming so proficient, and to them both it seemed, moreover, too crushing a blow to inflict upon William unless indeed there was found no doubt but that Edmund had a genuine vocation in the priesthood. Of her doubts Mrs. Froude wrote Newman. Her letter contains one of the few references in all the Froude papers to William's brother, Anthony, still looked upon as something of a black sheep because of his early heretical views.

I don't know why I should write to you, simply to say that I do not know how to feel about this resolution of Eddy's. I fear I am so weak minded that I can only feel at present sorrow for the great pain and disappointment it has caused to his father. Indeed the dear man has had blow upon blow since first I announced my intention of being a Catholic—and this last seems the heaviest of all—for he had just begun to find Eddy a thoroughly pleasant companion and with Eddy's excellent professional promise Wm felt he might look forward to his being a distinguished person. All this hope is of course now dispelled; and he has the additional pain of feeling that Eddy has left a career of honor and credit for one which (I fear) is looked on by him with dislike and disapprobation—and which he feels must place a gulf of separation between them for ever.

This is the more painful because evidently Wm had been the more agreeably surprised by finding Eddy's becoming a Catholic has not in any degree produced the separation which he anticipated. On the contrary they have been far more drawn together than they were before:—and Wm has often expressed himself to me as surprised to see how quickly Eddy catches his ideas and masters them—and often suggests improvements which had not occurred to Wm but which he sees to be judicious. All this makes this blow the more crushing—and I hardly know how we shall get on. The first time Wm spoke to me after your letter came, he was in a state of great excitement, but I can see that, since that, he has been trying to control himself. He has not opened the subject to Eddy,—and he (E) did not like to begin it, till he had heard from you. Wm is going to Salcombe to see Anthony, who is there, and *that* will do him no good! However I have advised Eddy to write him there and give him his reasons for wishing to be a Priest—(for Eddy finds writing easier than speaking) and he has just finished and sent off his letter. It is a very good one—so quiet and unenthusiastic in tone that I think

Wm will see he is not acting under the influence of excited feelings—also saying how much pain it gives him to do what his father disapproves etc etc. Of course Anthony will pick it to pieces, and encourage Wm in his disapproval—but I can't help it.

Setting aside my sorrow for Wm I own I cannot help thinking that Eddy is young to make such a decision for his future life. I wish he could have gone on till he was 20, preparing for his profession and then, if he still continued to feel as he does now, I should have resigned him more cheerfully—and we should have had time to make up our minds.[6]

To Edmund himself Newman wrote a most judicious letter pointing out the serious nature of the decision Edmund was contemplating and counselling delay because he felt that Edmund was acting under the influence of an emotional excitement unwisely induced by Father Suffield, who had come to the Oratory for the retreat.

The Oratory, B^m.
July 24, 1864.

My dear Eddie,

I got your letter here on my return last night. As I went up to Town, it struck me that it was hardly fair to leave you to break what Fr Suffield said to Papa; when I spoke to you, I thought it more manly and confiding in him that you should do so. But then, on further thought, it seemed to me that . . . . I was bound to write to Papa myself, lest there should be cowardice in me.

For myself, I can but repeat what I said. Almighty God calls the soul in various ways and reasons. It is very seldom that one can know at *once* that one is called. I think that time is generally necessary. This requires patience, and patience is very difficult. I do not see that you can know in three days that you have a vocation to the priesthood. But till you know,

[6] July 23, 1864.

your father has a call on you. If you were quite sure, you must
follow God. Again if papa says " I urge nothing "—then you
may at once follow that path which, even if it did not turn
out in the event to be your vocation, would, while you were
in it, be of great use to you, and which may turn out in the
event to *be* your vocation—but if papa said definitely " I wish
you to remain at home," or " I wish you to go to Oxford," I
do not think that you have that certainty about your vocation,
to warrant you to go against his wishes. All this has reference
to the *Priesthood*. But you speak of entering *religion*—this is
not what I understood you to say last Monday. I thought you
said a vocation to the Priesthood. A vocation to religion is a
very different thing. If it would be a difficulty to decide on
the Priesthood, much greater is the difficulty to decide on
religion. And I confess that your letter has frightened me in
this respect. Of course I understand there is a fulness of
divine grace which leads the soul to go right in the most
unusual courses—but we ought to be sure that we have it.
Ordinally speaking, ordinary means must co-operate with
grace. Ordinarily speaking, a greater imprudence could not
be committed than for you at your age to decide upon religion.
Recollect it is said that as many souls are lost by choosing
wrongly as in any other way. A man may be more easily lost
by becoming a religious when he is not called, as by not becoming one when he is. And from the difference of what you
said to me and write to me, I don't think you have a clear
idea of the difference between the *religious* and the ecclesiastical state. There are *various* opinions given by Catholic
writers on the subject of the religious state. Partly it depends
on countries and on the character of nations. Again, regulars
are inclined to take one view,—secular priests another. I trust
I never should keep a soul back from God who was called to
religion, but I have known so many try and fail, that I am
always glad to see a person slow in determining—(a person
who tries and fails may do himself great harm) and when
ultimately a person waits and does *not* become a religious,
though I know some persons will say " You see he has *lost*
his vocation by waiting," it is quite as open to say, and some-

times I *should* say "You see he has *found out* what *is* his real vocation by waiting."

I should recommend your going about your direct duties whatever they are—and reading *obvious* religious books—but not thinking at all about any religious vocation or order (anyhow you must go, not by books, but by a director).

I have written hastily, but I hope intelligibly.

Ever yrs aff[ly]
John H. Newman.

To Mrs. Froude Newman also wrote of his distress at Edmund's unfortunate decision. With the greatest delicacy he put forth the two duties facing him, that to the Church and that to his friends. In this case his heart lay more with his friends and consequently he advised against any decision to enter immediately upon the ecclesiastical state.

The O[r] B[m]
July 24, 1864.

My dear Mrs Froude,

I have told Eddy to shew you my letter to him, but can't help writing to you too.

Deeply do I grieve for this additional trouble to William and you; but God's will be done. I would not tell Eddy of Fr Suffield's coming, not being quite satisfied about it—and before he went into retreat, I cautioned him—but I was not satisfied after, more than before it.

I understood Eddy when he spoke to me last Monday that Fr Suffield spoke of the *ecclesiastical state*—but by his letter of to-day I find he speaks of the *religious* state. Does he know the real difference between them? certainly he so speaks as if he thought them about the same, that is, he does not know enough about them to be able to have any view at present on the subject.

He speaks of setting about to read about "religious orders" —all this afflicts me. It is not the way, I think, to find God's will. He says that St Alfonso speaks of the danger of losing a vocation. Then I say seriously, there is danger in *reading* St Alfonso, (as well as there may be in reading the Bible). The truth is there is as great danger in taking up a religious vocation when one has *not* one, as of neglecting such vocations when one *has* one.

I do not doubt at all he will bear this in mind. He is quite docile—but he must choose whom he will go by—anyhow he must not go by books. He may go by Fr Suffield, if he thinks it is God's will—or not—But Fr Suffield did not come here to fix vocations. Eddy says he came up here to *ask* Fr Suffield whether he had a vocation—does he mean " to the priesthood " or " to a religious order "? I can't help thinking, that the idea of a religious order did not come into his mind till the retreat.

You will ask me what I think should be done. From what Eddy says, I suppose Wm has decided not to send him to Oxford. This I take for granted. I think that Wm will fully expect that in the event he will *not* go on with any secular profession, and that Wm will naturally say " I have no wish merely to educate him for the Catholics."

If this is so, next comes the question, when should he be? The chance is that, *wherever* he goes, he will be committed to that place *when* he goes; and I should not wish him at his age committed *anywhere*. He really must *not* commit himself. The idea distresses me.

Well, I think he must first get his father's wish. *If* his father said " I wish you to engage in this or that," I think he must do so. But he says that papa " recommends that I should now wait at home *till* I can determine to *what community* or order to go." Oh how unreal this is! How can I let a poor boy be forced into making a choice *now*? Not that Wm means it—but it is the consequence of what Eddy has (from ignorance) told his father.

At the moment I do not know what to advise—and I would rather think more about it—and hear from you.

I grieve to trouble you, if this letter will do so—but I am in great trouble about it myself.

I think he was wrong (poor fellow) in asking Fr Suffield the question and not me. He might go to Fr Suffield for a retreat but not to make up his course of life. I think he should have asked me *whether* he might ask Fr Suffield. But it was a natural mistake. Unless he had distinctly said that he *came* to ask Fr Suffield I should have thought that Fr Suffield began —but Fr Suffield could not help answering according to his own view, if Eddy asked him. Pray God it may all turn to good.

Ever yours aff^{ly}
John H. Newman.

Froude's own objection was largely on the grounds of intellectual principle since such a step seemed to him tantamount to a profession of belief in certainty and in permanence (in this case of a particular state of mind), and what brought greater pain than the loss he naturally felt at his son's proposed entrance upon the priesthood was this transgression of a primary law of intelligent action—the preservation of a residuum of " sacred doubt."

Newman's objections, coming of course from other sources, were added to those of Froude, and while he could not conscientiously discourage Edmund entirely from pursuing his plan, he maintained so coldly critical an attitude in discussing the idea that Edmund could but feel the serious consequence of his intention and hesitate at the prospect before him. With the desire to alleviate as much as possible Froude's acute distress, Newman wrote to explain more fully the circumstances leading up to Edmund's plans and his own part in them.

The Oratory, B^m.
July 28, 1864.

My dear William,

Though I was seriously distressed that you should suffer so

much, there was nothing in your letter for anyone to take offence at. And I was rather amazed at Eddy myself. His letters to you have in great measure cleared the matter up, tho' I am still expecting a letter from him and cannot write absolutely, any more than you could to him, without knowing more of his feelings and wishes—and I half fear I have shown my state of mind to him, and that that is the reason why he does not write.

The reasons which he gives to you were news to me, though I see at once they are the real ones. I suppose he could not all at once bring these out to me—and I cannot but feel great sympathy and pity for a poor boy wishing to flee the world because it is so sweet—and I am sure you do too.

Nothing can shew both the naturalness and the confusion of his idea better, than the way he has mixed up, as I think, two things quite distinct—the religious state and the ecclesiastical state. His one object is to leave secular pursuits, and he does not care how. When he spoke to me, I understood him to be desiring the ecclesiastical state, and to be aiming at orders, the priesthood. To that effect I wrote to you. In his letter from Elmsliegh, he writes to me about a *religious* order—as if it were the same thing. His mother writes to me about his wish for the *priesthood*—and to you he writes (somewhere) of the ecclesiastical *or* religious state, (or some much words). In truth his one object is to leave the world. . .

I have just heard from your wife to say that Eddy is going to write to me. I suppose he hardly knows what to say, and, if his letter does not come before evening, I shall write to him. The notion of his going to try his vocation as a regular *at once*, is to me simply preposterous—and I never will give my consent to it. It would, in a year perhaps, determine his calling for life. As time went on, he might bitterly regret what he had done, and find that he must put the regret from him because he was under a vow. His life might be miserable. Of course it *might* turn out very well—and so it may turn out well if a child engaged himself to be married; but we must go by our best judgment. Nor could I trust the Religious fathers, under whom he put himself for trial and decision, unless I knew them most intimately—because of course they would be biassed as well as he, and, unless they were men of great caution and experience, would consider the devoutness and religiousness of youth the sufficient token of a vocation for themselves.

The notion then of his trying a religious vocation at once, I should quite put aside. As to an ecclesiastical vocation, if I understand his mother's expressions in the letter just come, I don't think he contemplates that, as distinct from the other—but I cannot make out. However, I look at it very differently. First, it seems to me in many cases the first step *towards* a religious vocation—therefore in admitting the idea of it in his case, I am saving myself from the danger of quenching his desire for a religious vocation, if it really comes from God. He would be proceeding by steps, not per saltum. 2. The listening to the idea determines nothing *at once*—for the irrevocable engagement to the ecclesiastical profession is not incurred by minor orders, but by the subdiaconate—which he could not receive before he is 21, and need not of course then—and so there is no reason, even if he *had* a calling to the priesthood that he should not go to Oxford.

In saying all this I am speaking as his director, and I should give (if I could safely) this advice, viz. go on just as if no thoughts had come across you—go on with your secular studies—go to Oxford or Cambridge if papa wishes, and see where you find yourself when you have taken your degree. If *then*, you deliberately consider that God wishes you to be a Priest, nay or a religious, I have nothing to say against it—or rather, I thank God.

And for yourself, my dear William, I think you would be in the position of many a parent besides yourself, who wishes his son to succeed him in his Bank, or a fine profitable business, and he *will* go into a profession or into the army—or who wants his son to marry a certain lady, and he *will* fix his affections on some one else. I do not think you would have any right to complain, *because* Eddy would be a *man*. And as to his pledging himself by a vow, so does every Anglican Clergyman on his ordination, and it is attended with serious civil disabilities—as they find full well when they (Angl. Clerg.) become Catholics; moreover, when a man is old enough to vow to love for ever a certain woman, I think he is old enough to vow celibacy.

There is only one difficulty which I should find on my side in *insisting* on Eddy going to the University (i. e., if *you* wished it) and it is what you speak of yourself when you allude to his being " placed in a perpetual conflict with himself." *As time went on*, I might find that it was the lesser of two evils for him to make up his mind about the Priesthood or Religious Order sooner than the date I have mentioned.

You must recollect that he is quite at *liberty*, if he *chooses*, to leave *me* and to take Fr Suffield for his director. I think he *ought* not to do so—and, if he remains with me, I shall insist on his having no communication with Fr Suffield. A soul cannot have two physicians at once. He never ought to have consulted Fr Suffield on the point. I shall tell him so—but he is so distressed just now, that I must not wound him. Please do not hint this to him.

Thank you for letting me see the correspondence, which I return. I think his letters very good ones—and yours a very good one, and I trust and pray that, where everyone wishes what is right, everything will go well; though (if I am right in thinking he will not ultimately depart from at least his *ecclesiastical* direction) there must be in the event pain to you.

Ever yours most affect[ly]
John H. Newman.

Mrs. Froude kept him informed as to the reception of the news at home. Froude's unhappy state of mind is only too easily imagined from the brief lines of his wife's letter.

July 30, 1864.

Dear Fr. Newman,

. . . Eddy read your letter this morning and showed it to me. He sees perfectly the justice of what you say—and thinks it both kind and wise. One thing only you have mistaken, as, I believe, *his* letter will set right, he did *not* " come to Edgbaston with the intention of consulting Fr S. about his vocation."

. . . Your letter to Wm came most opportunely yesterday evening, when all the young folks were gone on an expedition to Dartmouth and Dartington—and Wm and I were alone. He showed me the letter and talked about it saying it was excellent common sense as well as most kind. But he sighed a great deal as we walked about the garden to-gether—and said much which there is no use repeating but which made me feel what a gulf there is between us. It is always extraordinary to me (seeing what excellent sense and judgment he has on most subjects) that in talking of Catholic matters, he does talk such nonsense, such as " there can be nothing in the system of spiritual direction unless every director is infallible," as if one ought never to go to a doctor unless the doctor is infallible. But I always comfort myself he talks more unreasonably to *me,* than he would to anyone else,—or even than he thinks. It is more by way of relief from the pain which oppresses him (just as one groans or cries out) and wives are meant to be beasts of burden. So I do not in the least mean to complain. But I do wish he could see things differently.

. . . Wm has said nothing but I hope he will wish him to go to Oxford or Cambridge . . .

As for Edmund himself, when he had soberly considered the magnitude of his project, he was considerably mortified at his unwise haste in disclosing the state of his mind before it was properly made up. He wrote to Newman confessing his shame at the pain, so largely unnecessary, which he had occasioned, and begged Newman to suggest penances, in addition to those which he himself contemplated, which might help in a measure to correct the wrong he had done. This Newman did, at the same time taking the opportunity to review the whole situation and to point out again the fact that there was at least a possibility that Edmund might sin as much in entering upon a vocation unless such were without doubt the will of God, as he would in foregoing the course were he indubitably called to it. Newman's advice, worldly as it might seem if judged narrowly from an ecclesiastical point of view, really sprang from the most devout wish best to further both the cause of the Church and the ultimate welfare of his young friend. Broad, too, was his outlook for Edmund's education, for he was only too aware of how limited in scope might be Edmund's development if he deprived himself of an education such as could be procured nowhere else save at Oxford or Cambridge.

The Oratory, B^m.
August 3, 1864.

My dear Eddy,

Your letter is a very good one, and perfectly reasonable. I suppose I have answered most of it in my letter which crossed it.

1. I certainly think you *should* have some definite mortification. From my own fault, I daresay, I did not understand your wish for me till now. It is always advisable in such cases as you describe your own to be. The anxiety is to fix on one which is fitting—which may neither be a burden on your conscience nor interfere with your duties to others, and yet answer its purpose.

I do not know how to mention anything at once;—1. because I do not know what you do already. 2. next because it ought to be something which suits you. I will put down on a separate paper two or three penances, which you might choose from, or use as suggestions for others which I do not happen to mention.

2. I think it would be distinctly wrong in you to try your vocation for *religion* at once. You *must* try it in a particular place and order—and places and orders are toto caelo differ-

ent. Nothing is more common among women (who more often try their vocation than men) than to try in a wrong community, and to get disheartened altogether, and to leave a religious vocation which they might have had, had they tried in the right place. And among men it occurs not unfrequently too. Great deliberation then is necessary as regards the place of attempting, lest vocations be quenched.

Another danger is this, lest a postulant and novice, being young, with warm affections and religious earnestness, should have all the signs of vocation and take the vows, and then after a while fall into a state of tepidity, which *may* indeed only be a fault of natural weakness and a re-action of mind which is to be resisted as a temptation, but on the other hand may quite as easily be the result of that spiritual constitution which God has given him, and such, that, if it had shown itself in him *while* he was a novice, might have made clear that, without any fault of his, he had *no* vocation for a religious state at all. Certainly, I think I see men who have made serious mistakes in becoming religious suddenly. Of course there are always two ways of explaining the failure—it made be said " he *fell* from his vocations "—or—" he *never* had a vocation " as this applies to an ecclesiastical vocation as well as to a religion, I will instance it in the case of Mr Conelly, an American convert. He separated from his wife; she became a religious (and is still a very good one—she is Mother Sup^r of the St Leonard's Convent) he a Priest. Then, he found he had mistaken his vocation—wished to get back his wife—left the Church and is now an Irvingite. He *could* have got her back *legally*—and there was great trouble about it. Mr Sibthorp may be taken as another case in point.

Then again, when the event does not shew it, yet one's own previous experience of individuals may lead to the same conclusion. I have known persons suddenly become religious, who (I am quite sure) were not fit *except* by quasi-miracle or a real miracle. Such a gracious act of Providence there *may* have been: but, when I see cases before my eyes, of false vocations (as I think), from the *event*, and therefore know there *are* such things, it is natural for me to fear that in the cases I am immediately speaking of, there is not miracle, but hasty decisions—and I look on gravely and anxiously to see what will come of it. But even if no *scandal* came of it, I should not be at my ease—because there is a dreadful case supposable of a soul under vows which he does not visibly break, but which enter like iron into his soul; and though, of course there [is] provision in the Church by which such vows may be dispensed with and souls set free, yet such a dispensation (it stands to reason) is a very serious matter and cannot occur every day, but requires extraordinary circumstances. Again, another case, really not uncommon and very sad, is when young women (who are in the world) deliberately, without their confessor's leave or knowledge, make vows of perpetual celibacy. Then perhaps, they repent of what they have done, and their confessors can do nothing to help them. I would not say all this to everyone—but I know you are a prudent boy, and I wish you gravely and continually to pray God, that you may be *taught* His Will as regards you. For we must persevere in prayer, if we would learn it.

3. I think it likely that you *have* a vocation to the priesthood—by which I mean that a vocation to a religious life is so much rarer than a vocation to the ecclesiastical state, that the latter is more easy to believe. As to the religious state, to take one particular, a very holy regular Jesuit once said to me at Rome, "No one knows what it is to be in *the absolute power* of another who has not experience of it." He indeed was called to it, yet he *felt* it—but he said what he said to caution me and others from acting hastily. Therefore I say I see nothing in you of a vocation to the religious state, but what a number of persons have who have no vocation to it at all, for they are not slight tokens which are the real evidence of it—but, as to the ecclesiastical state, it is no difficulty to me to believe that your present wish *may* be the incipient token of a vocation for *it*. Still, you are yet a boy—and the question is whether this token, whatever be its just value, is so strong and clear as to be a justification of your acting upon it against your father's wish. I do not deny that it might be so strong and clear—nay, nor that there might be

a token of a *religious* vocation strong enough, to justify or to require you to follow it out at once. I don't see that you *have* such strong evidence of a vocation.

Well then, as to the ecclesiastical vocation, moreover, even if you had one, *that* would not interfere with your going to a University, unless there was a great danger of residence at a University causing you to lose it. I do not think it need, even if you had one. On the contrary, I think University education may make you so useful as a Priest, that, though you had one, I should be glad of your having that education. Moreover, I think it may be a good test, whether you have a vocation, to see if you can persevere in your desire for one, through your residence. I do not see that such residence need interfere at all with a vocation, if a youth had one.

Ever yours very affect[ly]
John H. Newman.

Newman was unwilling to allow even the appearance of jesuitical conduct on his own part, and he carefully informed Froude of every detail concerning Edmund's situation.

The Oratory, B[m]
Aug[st] 8, 1864.

My dear William,

I will not speak on the subject of your distress, because I may seem to have no business to do so. All I can say is that Eddy's inclination is not my doing. No one can answer for a boy's mind, and no one can turn him at his [age] no one can control his ultimate [intentions]. One can but influence him for a time, and *then* he must be his own master, and he must decide for himself whether that influence has succeeded in the interval to determine his decision or not.

When he spoke to me the other day, I might have put off the question (as I did) and *also* have said nothing to you about it. I might have said nothing to you till such time, if the time ever came, when he actually had determined on orders. I might have said to him "Don't tell your father your thoughts, go to Oxford as he wishes—if you ultimately make up your mind for the ecclesiastical state, then tell him—but give him the chance of having no annoyance, by not telling him now when it is uncertain." Then perhaps the idea of Orders would have died out of his mind, and you would never have known the difficulty.

But neither he nor I felt that such a course was possible. I did not see I had any right to keep you in ignorance of what was going on in his mind. Supposing, after being 4 years at Oxford, his mind had been made up to follow up his wish to take Orders, and it had then come out that he had spoken to me on the subject before he went there. I think you would have had good reason to be much hurt, considering the expense which you had been put to for him at the University. Of course a residence there would have only been so much gain to him when he became an ecclesiastic, but it would be sharp practice in me to have allowed it.

I doubt not he will say to you, if he has not already, that he wishes to do just what you decide about Oxford, a Tutor etc.—but I have not liked to press him strongly, for he seemed to me disturbed, and I thought it best to give him time to recover himself. Many a Protestant boy with his strong feelings would have in a headstrong way acted upon them. He has been saved from this conduct by his own good principle, and the *influence* you have over him: and partly by his religious advisers.

Ever yrs aff^{ly}
John H. Newman.

Edmund informed his father and Newman that he wished to persevere in his intention to become a priest, but he agreed to postpone any final decision until after he had completed his education and should then be better equipped to decide his future course. Everything turned out, eventually, as Newman thought it might, and Edmund came to see that his vocation was to serve

God not in religious but in secular ways. Newman's letter of August 12, 1864, concluded the correspondence over this affair.

My dear William,

I am sure there is no one who can ask so little, as a Father, as you do. You are a great deal more than fair, you are most kind. And really, though it does no good to say so, I am really quite pierced, when I think how much you must suffer. And if I have said a single word, against my will, which you felt I need not have said, I am very sorry for it.

I won't say that Eddy's communication to me took me by surprise, for I had already, as I told you, some anxious suspicion on the subject—but it is nothing but the fact to say, that it was very unwelcome to me—unwelcome, except so far as my duty calls on me to rejoice that God brings a soul into His more immediate service. When I received Protestant Orders, I believed no state of life so excellent as that of the Christian ministry—and much more do I think so now. Putting this aside, it is to me a simple trouble that Eddy is not giving himself to the profession you intend for him.

I wish to press upon him that, if there is a danger of his swerving from God's will by not going into Orders, so he may be swerving from it by going into Orders. And I hope he will go to Oxford resolved to make the most of his time and opportunities—and you, better than I, know what good foundation there is for this hope.

Ever yours most affect^{ly}
John H. Newman.

Edmund did not go up to either Oxford or Cambridge, but, on completing his course at the Oratory School, entered at once upon a scientific career and continued to assist Froude in private investigations. In later life he was attached to the British Admiralty and made further contributions to naval designing which won him honors only second to his father's. He died in 1924.

VI
FINAL CORRESPONDENCE

VI

FINAL CORRESPONDENCE

THE following years brought to Froude some measure of the peace which had been so long denied him. His scientific experiments were meeting with a success he had never dared to expect, and from naval engineering he began to turn his thoughts to the conquest of a still more difficult medium, the air. At the time of his death he was making observations on the flight of birds with a view to propounding physical laws pertaining to their motion. In these experiments he was helpfully assisted by Edmund, and there never again arose the question of a religious vocation. After the trying year of 1864 Newman too emerged on the heights where he could pause to survey the fruits of his toil, at last with some satisfaction.

The correspondence of the two men took on a softer tone. Nearly all had been said on both sides that could be said. For Froude there remained but to reiterate his steadfast adherence to that type of belief so removed from the Oratorian's. And Newman, though temporarily exhausted by the strain of writing his *Apologia,* had progressed almost to the point where he could make explicit the argument for religious belief which had for so many years been taking shape in his mind. There had yet to come only the spark of inspiration necessary to release his stored-up thought, and within a short time, while resting in the mountains above Montreux, there flashed upon him the method of beginning his exposition. During the intervening years, before Newman had completed the *Grammar of As-*

sent, the two exchanged letters, now rather more brief than before, upon the events which made up the daily course of life.

In the autumn of 1864 their letters were in a manner a valedictory to the intense arguments that had filled the earlier years. But the scientific mode of thought, as well as the increasingly threatening aspect of science toward established religious opinion, was becoming more and more widespread. From being a province familiar only to men of especial cast of mind, science, and its implications, was beginning to permeate literature of a popular sort.

In September, 1864, Fitzjames Stephen wrote for *Fraser's Magazine* an article, " Dr. Newman's Apologia," [1] in which he suggested some of the scientific objections to Newman's argument, pointing out that the " considerations which finally decided him [Newman—to become a Catholic] were of a sentimental rather than of a rational kind." [2] He specifically attacked Newman's view of accumulating probabilities as making for certainty, and showed how they tended rather in the opposite direction, and concluded that " This misapprehension of the nature of probability vitiates the whole of Dr. Newman's theory." [3] He held, as did Froude, that " It is the first of intellectual duties always to reserve for ourselves a liberty of doubting on every question whatever, however firm may be our present belief, however sacred the matter to which it applies." [4] Froude felt that the article stated his own view, " with a vigor and clearness which is quite beyond my power," and it was, therefore, with the hope of justifying his view by the corroborative testimony of

---

[1] Vol. LXXX, pp. 265-303.
[2] P. 269.   [3] P. 269.   [4] P. 292.

WILLIAM FROUDE

other prominent thinkers (among them Sir Charles Lyell) that Froude wrote Newman calling his attention to the article and its bearing upon their past discussions.

Elmsleigh,
29th Sept. 1864

My dear Newman,

If you are not wearied outright by the subject, I wish to persuade you to read an article on the Apologia in Fraser's Magazine for September—it is written by Mr. Fitzjames Stephen a Barrister of high standing, son of Sir. J. Stephen who was so long Under Secy for the Colonies.

I send by book post a copy of this Number of Fraser—only if it bores you, do not scruple to send it back unread.

The part of the Article which makes me wish to induce you to read it, is that which relates to the application of the proposition "To us probability is the guide of life." So far as it relates to the question between yourself and Mr. Kingsley—and indeed perhaps throughout the Article, there is a roughness of tone which gives it an unpleasantness even where the general view adopted is not harsh. But the weighty nature of the fundamental questions involved in the light and the law of probability as the guide of life renders, I think, a mere tinge of roughness in the tone with which it is treated, comparatively immaterial. And the reason why I especially wish you to read the article is that in the part to which I refer the substance of the views which the writer expresses is more nearly that which I always feel a wish to express, than anything which I have elsewhere fallen in with. And it is here expressed with a vigour and clearness which is quite beyond my power. Moreover I know that, whatever loose talk many men of undoubted scientific ability may indulge in about the certainty of the conclusions to which science leads, I know that all the really high cast minds, which are engaged in the advancement of science and also pursue it in that really philosophical spirit which alone serves to consolidate the advances made, *all* treat their own conclusions with a skepticism as profound, and as corroding as that with which they treat Theology.

The scientific propositions which are regarded as most certain, are those the probability of which *is being* most continually tested and found to stand the test. I will not attempt to say more in my clumsy way of what is much better said by the reviewer. I should not have said so much, had not this perpetually reacting skepticism of Scientific Men, as it affects the Conclusions of Science, been recently very strongly impressed on my mind by some conversation I had with Sir Charles Lyell the other day in the train, on the Road from Bath to London.

I am not a good reporter, or I would have tried to set down the substance of what struck me in his remarks, but I cannot refrain from noticing the impression which they made on me though it may perhaps render you suspicious of the fairness of that impression when I add that it is in entire accordance with the views which have been for years growing on me and which I have invariably expressed when a discussion has arisen such as to make room for them.

Newman replied the next day:

The Oratory, B^m
Sept. 30, 1864.

My dear William,

I had already got and partially read the article in Frazer. I recognized at once that it expressed your view, which I have not forgotten from the time that you told me of it. Whether I shall ever bring out my own view as that article brings out the contrary one, remains just as it was. On the one hand I scarcely ever have written without an urgent or compulsive force applied to me—on the other hand it is of course a matter which requires great and careful investigation. Though I have no doubt in my own view, I feel the same diffidence of my power to bring it out as you do of yours. I don't know whether many persons feel like me, and I seem to myself never to be able to do to-day what I happened to do yesterday.

I know nothing about the future though I know well that I should like to write on the subject in question—most especially like and desire and pray to do so.

As I *have* the Frazer, I have not taken yours from its cover, and would send it at once back, unless it were in appearance ungracious to do so. I dare say it is your only copy.

There is (I say it in confidence) a chance of our having the Mission in Oxford. If so, I should be necessarily brought there from time to time myself—and this might force me to write on these subjects. I hope you and your wife are well.

Ever yrs most affect^{ly}
John H. Newman,
of the Oratory.

Froude's reply to Newman's acknowledgment was the last occasion on which he may be said to have exerted any influence upon Newman's thinking. He had long felt what Sir Charles Lyell said so aptly, that anything Newman would have to say after mature consideration would be of the greatest value even if it could not be expected in any large degree to alter the *status quo*. For the last time he urged upon Newman the necessity of remaining open to every adverse probability, but it was, however, to the all important point of the illative sense, as it was later to be called, that Froude's caveat was most centrally directed. His admission of the possibility of an almost supernatural faculty in the mind capable of judging infallibly seems to have weighed heavily, for this point did prove, eventually, to be the keystone of Newman's system. But Froude so hedged the admission about with difficulties that Newman was never able to overcome them, to Froude's satisfaction at least, and the final argument of the *Grammar of Assent* was, from the scientific viewpoint, unconvincing. Part of Froude's letter follows:

I am glad [he wrote] your attention had been attracted by the Fraser article, and I wish very much you could be driven to answer it. Conclusive as the arguments in which its view rests appear to me to be I feel sure that the counter view which so entirely satisfies you must be capable of very powerful and very clear justification, and you are of all men the one to undertake the exposition of this. I suppose that many persons as well as myself used to think of you in the days when the Church of England fabric began to look shaky, with a feeling which (in a manner) inevitably brought to mind " Si Pergame dextra etc., etc." and the same feeling still survives.

The Apologia has been very much read by men of Science and with a feeling of great interest, a feeling which couples the perception of extreme power of mind in the writer with an anxious and (wondering) curiosity to know how he substantiates the bridge by which he steps so freely from the state of doubt which (as they feel) inevitably attaches to these results of probabilities, to the state of absolute certainty which he seems to substitute for this. I travelled with Sir C. Lyell the other day to London on his return from the British Association Meeting at Bath, and without my leading the conversation in that direction the subject came naturally to the surface, and he expressed the feeling which I have mentioned not indeed as having a misgiving that you would be able to turn the stream back but as knowing that what you would have to say would deserve very serious consideration.

It will be curious indeed if you should be brought to write on the subject from Oxford.

It seems to me that the question has to be dealt with at two successive steps or levels. First, is the principle that belief is always to be tempered by or to leave room for, doubt when it is founded on probability, the rightful and logical application of " Probability " as the " guide of life " in relation *to life in its ordinary human aspect.*

Second, supposing the first question answered in the affirmative is the principle equally applicable in dealing with those probabilities on which religious belief is founded.

At least it seems to be a tenable view, a priori, that men are intended to deal differently with their conclusions when these lead up into Religion from that way in which they deal with conclusions relating to the ordinary affairs of life—as if instinct were to guide them in one case, logic in the other; though an abundant crop of intractable difficulties arise when one attempts to reduce the distinction into a rule of practical application, and though your grounds of demur seem to make themselves felt towards the view itself, when its corollaries are looked into. For in the first place, it is extremely difficult if not impossible to draw a clear and available line between the probabilities which lead up into Religion and those which belong to Common life so interwoven the two classes of questions are, when one really looks into them. And in the second place, if the distinction is regarded as sound, it seems at once necessary to assume that men are gifted with an instinctive faculty which enables them to perceive with certainty the facts of a supernatural occurrence, and to recognize it as super-natural at once and by a conscious act of unerring recognition instead of by intricate (and to a man of science impossible) process of determining in the first place that it is not natural.[5]

Newman and Froude began to turn at last from these protracted arguments to more personal matters, and their letters ceased to be of so purely a philosophical and argumentative nature. As the Oxford days became more and more a distant memory, many of Newman's other Protestant friends renewed the ties of friendship which had once bound them so closely. In 1865 Newman had the great pleasure of seeing R. W. Church and Frederick Rogers. Newman described, with some irony, their meeting to Mrs. Froude.

. . . I was with Rogers for two days on occasion of the Archbishop's consecration. Church came up to meet me. We

[5] October 8, 1864.

had a very pleasant time. It was always Rogers' fault, yet it is difficult to find fault with a high standard. But he seems to me softened with years. And then the development of liberalism, and the great divisions in the Anglican Church may make him more patient. His note of the Church is sanctity; and he has been accustomed to apply it savagely, nothing could be more easy and familiar than his manner with me now. My surmise is, that he thinks me a profoundly sceptical thinker, who, determined on not building on an abyss, have, by mere strength of will, bridged it over, and built upon my bridge—but that my bridge, like Mahomet's Coffin, is self suspended, by action of the will—but I may be putting it too strong. He himself is not nearly so sceptical as I had feared. I like Lady Rogers very much.[6]

His many friends, Catholic and Protestant alike, continued to write about their problems, and Newman devoted more and more of his time to answering, often at great length, the questions put to him, sometimes by total strangers. Though his own life had become more easy and his belief if possible even more assured, Newman was none the less keenly aware of the persistence with which doubts could assail less settled minds. Of the seventy thousand letters on file at the Oratory in Edgbaston, a large number are of the years immediately following the publication of the *Apologia,* and relate to the questions of scepticism and faith. Among the many who wrote to Newman was young Edmund Froude, who was now beginning to fulfill his splendid promise as a scientist. Nothing could be more patiently reassuring than his reply to Edmund's perplexities concerning the Holy Sacraments.

. . . Then, as to your doubts, it is wonderful if they never

[6] August 7, 1865. A portion of this letter is given in Ward, *Life,* II, 90.

had come upon you. I have expected you would have them all along. It is impossible that a young and opening mind, such as yours, should not have them sooner or later. There are large questions which cannot be taken in all at once—and they must come as questions before they admit of answers. They are like plus and minus quantities, equal to each other severally, in an equation. The plus come first, I mean, objections—then come the minus, the answers; and the equation is left at the end, as it began. This subject is beautifully treated, poetically not algebraically, in the Hymn in the Christian Year on the Epiphany.

God is not a hard master—nor is the Church severe—you have an honest heart, and desire to do what is right. Sacraments are not snares—privileges are not burdens. Put off your trouble as much as you can, put yourself into God's hands and be patient. I shall be glad to see you at any time.

Ever yrs aff^{ly}
John H. Newman.[7]

Though the fervor of his letters diminished, Newman did not cease earnestly to hope that Froude himself might still be brought over to the Catholic Church. Others were induced to try what they could do in convincing him on purely logical grounds, and among those who made serious endeavors of this sort was Henry Wilberforce. About this attempt, Newman wrote to Mrs. Froude: " It is an anxious thing, but very interesting to me, to know what comes of Henry Wilberforce's letters." [8] One of the letters which Wilberforce wrote has been preserved among the Froude papers, but it contained no very persuasive arguments, nor indeed anything different from what Froude had for years been receiving.

The passing of time brought many changes that were

---

[7] April 20, 1866. [8] August 20, 1868.

strange indeed, and one in particular must have seemed very ironic to Froude. In 1870 Father Suffield, the priest who had done so much to turn Edmund's mind toward a religious vocation, renounced Catholicism. Newman wrote an account of the unpleasant affair to Mrs. Froude.

> The Oratory
> Aug 22. 1870
>
> My dear Mrs Froude,
>
> I have meant to write to you day after day—but it is not pleasant to say what had to be said.
>
> F^r Suffield has certainly given up Christianity—and calls himself a " Christian Theist "—that is, a Deist thinking Christianity has done good—something like the Hindoo Sem or the modern Unitarians. It is difficult to believe that this is the work of a moment, though he allows that the Definition has brought the matter to a head—but his account is that he has not believed the miracles of Scripture for these ten years. This of course is frightful, considering he has been giving missions all over the country—and would make one say one would believe no one in future except one's own personal friends—it would be an enormous trial to numbers—but the Dominicans deny it—say that he has had temptations, and that lately he has yielded to them. He seems to have given up his missions for some time and lived in retirement—however, last year he readily undertook to preach for us on St. Philip's day.
>
> Instead of coming here, he took lodgings in Birmingham—out of delicacy, saying he had made up his mind, and had no question to put before me. He goes talking all about and writing—and I never should be surprised at his writing to Eddie. He professes to have found out that the Jesuits etc etc are worldly people, and that they don't care for religion at Rome so much as for political objects. Mrs Wilberforce as well as her husband has been made quite ill by it.
>
> > Ever yrs aff^{ly}
> > John H Newman.

In 1870, at long last, Newman's great philosophical treatise appeared, dedicated to his friend Edward Bellasis. In the following summer Newman republished his articles in the *British Critic,* and, as in some measure to pay a debt of long standing, he wished to dedicate the volumes to Froude. First, however, he tactfully inquired of Mrs. Froude whether this would be acceptable to her husband.

I am publishing my Articles in the British Critic—with the addition of answers to such portions as are Anglican. They will form two volumes.

I want to dedicate them to William—but first before writing to ask him, I wish to be sure from you that he would like me to do so.

If he gives me his consent, I shall then send you the dedication to make sure that there is nothing in it which could displease him.[9]

Froude, however, felt constrained at first to decline the courtesy Newman wished to extend. He remained ever acutely sensitive of the differences separating his thought from Newman's, and he did not wish, by accepting Newman's offer, either to compromise his own position or to appear to be sailing under false colors. He replied to Newman's letter in his characteristic kindly way, pausing amid scientific analysis to quot classic periods learned long since in an English public school.

I have felt deeply the persistent affectionate regard for me of which it is but a fresh token that you should wish to dedicate to me the republication of your British Critic Articles. And what is there that I can say in reply but that both on that account and in remembrance of the eager and almost

[9] July 19, 1871.

passionate interest with which we used to look out for them and delight in them when they first appeared. What you have proposed would give me the greatest pleasure.

And yet there is something that I ought to say, I am always in fear lest I should be somehow sailing under false colours in your sight; I do not mean deliberately and with pretence but by allowing you somehow through your affection for me to think more of me and better of me as if somehow you were supposing that were you to probe me to the bottom you would find more solid ground for approbation, a more real root of what you would regard as "Faith" than a thorough search would in fact disclose, and to let you dedicate your book to me would be in some degree to take credit for possessing what I believe does not belong to me. I do not mean that I have disguised from you what I have come to think, or how I have come to think it, but I do think that I have [n]ever *so* acquainted you with it as to form an opinion of me uncolored by affectionate regard. It has never seemed necessary to do this, and on the contrary it has seemed almost as if it would be both "bumptious" and disrespectful, and indeed to one who is not master of his own ideas (has not framed them into something like a coherent and consistent whole) and who is not master of the art of explaining himself, it is a weary and hopeless task to attempt such an explanation. And except that I ought always to decline what I fancy to be your too favourable opinion of me it has seemed enough that I should let you know how far I have deviated not only from the Theological foundation but from the mode of dealing with Theological questions which used to guide me when you came to think well of me. I believe, indeed, I have before now told you how these foundations seemed to be shaken when grave differences arose between you and Mr. Keble on questions which you both regarded as of fundamental importance. I do not know that I could describe the character and this state better than in the words which Aneas used to describe the outset of his wanderings and the feeling with which he was launched into them; the words are so often in my mind that perhaps I shall quote them incorrectly (I think it is near 50 years ago that I first learned them).

> "Postquam res Asiae Priamique evertere gentem
> immeritam visum superis, ceciditque superbum
> Ilium et omnis humo fumat Neptunia Troia,
> diversa exsilia et desertas quaerere terras
> auguriis agimur divum, classemque sub ipsa
> Antandro et Phrygiae molimur montibus Idae,
> incerti quo fata ferant, ubi sistere detur."

Many of us were then started on our normal lines of thought, and have come to be *settled* in various phases of *unsettlement*. For myself I ought to say that the concluding line of the passage is definitely accepted by me as my normal condition of thought and the entire absence of certitude has long ceased to be painful to me or to be something which one should try to escape from as an evil.

There are others indeed who felt their own footing so surely that the shake didn't unsettle them and who whatever minor changes of defined belief they may have undergone they still hold to the old ground;—and when this firmness is a reality, when it seems to know its road and to pick its steps with clearness and judgment and to plant them with firm tread, it seems impossible to me not to regard it with a kind of reverence. Some such position Rogers appears to me to occupy, and if I have speculated before-hand on the name which would seem to me you could most fitly place where you have proposed to place mine, his is that which would have occurred to me.

You probably know his " locus " of thought better than I do, but I know myself better than you do, and however heartily I hold to every proof of your affection for me, yet if to perceive the realization of the fitness of things be one of the several grounds of solid satisfaction, it would give me more solid satisfaction to see his name on your title page than my own.

I am obliged to write very late and hurriedly, and I have to be in the Dockyard all tomorrow and probably the next day (about some experiment in which Eddy is most helpfully assisting me), and I must now finish.

> Believe me, Sir,
> Yours affectionately,
> W. Froude [10]

Newman had not for Rogers the sympathy and affection which had always bound him to Froude, and he could not agree that Roger's name would stand more fittingly at the head of his volumes. Consequently he wrote Froude again, in more detail, pressing him to reconsider.

> The Oratory
> July 29, 1871.

My dear William,

Thank you for your frank letter—I am sure you will continue to be so. Of course I wish to gratify myself in dedicating the volumes to you—but it would be no gratification to me, if I gave you even the shadow of pain or trouble. Therefore, as you are kind to me, you will be, please, most frank in this matter.

Say distinctly that you had rather not, and, though I shall be sorry, I shall be quite satisfied.

Perhaps I ought to have written to you direct—and then to have accompanied my petition by an explanation. I will do so now.

I publish 15 Essays in two volumes—some of them you must know, but not all. They run as follows. 1. Poetry. 2. Rationalism of Erskine and Abbot. 3. La Mennais. 4. Palmer's theology. 5. Epistles of St Ignatius. 6. Prospects of the Anglican Church. 7. Anglo-American Church. 8. Lady Huntingdon. 9. Catholicity of the Anglican Church. 10. Protestant idea of Antichrist. 11. Milman's Christianity. 12. Hildebrand. 13. Private Judgment. 14. John Davison. 15. John Keble.

[10] July, 1871.

WILLIAM FROUDE

Some of them are defences of Anglicanism. I could not then consistently republish them, without stating why I was now dissatisfied with them. Therefore the work has *two* sides —two sides of the controversy.

Hence, I could not dedicate it to Rogers—and, feeling this, last year I dedicated to him my two (Anglican) Essays on Miracles.

And in the sketch of dedication to you which I have drawn up in case you consent, I say,

"Whatever be your judgment of portions of their contents, which are not always in agreement with each other, you will, I know, accept them readily, when offered to you as the expression, such as it is, of their author's wish to connect his name with yours." This will meet your fear of your sailing under false colours.

However, I will enclose the whole Dedication as I sent it to your wife, and the Preface, which in a way anticipates a portion of your letter, though your case is *quite different*.

Ever yours aff'ly

John H. Newman.

Mrs. Froude was, as usual, the medium through which William corresponded with Newman, and she described her husband's reactions to the offer of the dedication, and gave at the same time her own view of the trials which had attended them through so many years.

You will have heard from W^m (so he tells me) and I hope you will have understood from his letter, that he will be really gratified if you carry out your kind intention; although he has scruples about accepting it (as I knew he would have) feeling that it would be (so to say) "sailing under false colors."

I think myself that he (W^m) is under a mistake in thinking that you do not understand or appreciate "the degree to which he has diverged, not only from your views, but from your principles of arriving at views."

I believe from what you have said when we have talked on the subjects, that you *do* understand him certainly. It seems to me that W^m is utterly removed from the common run of sceptics; and his mistakes appear to me to proceed in great measure from crankiness, and a sort of over-scrupulousness. But indeed, whatever they are, you know the worst of them, *that* I am convinced; and so, I do not see, why, if you kindly wish to dedicate your book to him he need have any scruples about it. Indeed he said as much in his letters to me,—viz.: that if, after reading what he has said, you still adhere to your intention, he would be very glad to have it done,—and he knows what a *very great pleasure* it would be to us all, and an affectionate remembrance of Hurrell. I do not at all agree with him that "it would be more appropriate for you to dedicate your book to Sir F Rogers." Of course, there is no doubt that he (Sir F. R.) has "held on more to the old ideas and modes of thought" than W^m. But in spite of that I should say that Sir F. was infinitely more averse to Catholicism than W^m. His (R's) own doubtful position (from which W^m has, to a certain extent, emancipated himself) makes it necessary for him to throw stones at us;—whereas W^m always allows that Catholicism is the legitimate development of dogmatic belief; and so far as he understands us he does us full justice, which I cannot say is the case with Sir F. Rogers. . . .

I feel quite sure that W^m will not object to your saying "amid many trials of friendship."

As far as I understood him (I have not seen him since) he meant that, in whatever trials he had suffered (viz.: from our leaving him) you had done all you could to soften them. I know he thinks *that*—he has always said it. But of course he knows well that we have all been (so to say) under your influence, without your being an active agent in the matter,—and there is no doubt it has been a trial to his friendship for you: and I think what you propose saying is most true and appropriate. I do not think you need have the least scruple in saying it, because his only objection has arisen from the fear that it would imply any diminution of his affection for you.

This I am saying without any communication with him—but

you will probably hear from him in answer to the letter I forwarded yesterday.[11]

In his reply to Newman's second letter Froude wrote in a single paragraph a tribute, comparable to Matthew Arnold's, among the most sincere and the most generous Newman ever received. In it Froude spoke not only for himself but for generations of Oxford men now long since down from the banks of the Isis.

Indeed throughout it is I who have been the debtor, and even whenever and wherever I have in opinions or modes of thought been not with you but against you, and I suppose I ought to say against Hurrell also (though his probable mental course had he lived to these days has seemed to me more problematical) it has seemed somehow I have owed the power of thinking and of judging and above all the sense of responsibility to something which you and he taught me. There never has been a time when if I have been among those whose judgments I have thought well of or whose opinions I have been inclined to agree with, however at variance with yours, it has not added to the readiness with which I have been listened to and served in a sense, to give weight to anything I have had to say, if I have casually mentioned that I have been your pupil and was still counted among your friends.[12]

Mrs. Froude gave Newman final assurance of the pleasure William would take in having Newman's book dedicated to him.

I must write you a few lines because I heave heard to-day from W^m from Portsmouth and he seems rather anxious with regard to his letters to you, about the dedication, fearing you might have imagined he wrote coldly, when (he said) he was really so much gratified at your wishing to do it. "But then I am sure he over-rates me, I have always felt so."

Then he ended, "I wish you could tell him (for I don't

[11] August 1, 1871.   [12] July 31, 1871.

like to write again) that I should be really pleased to have it done if, after what I have said, he still wishes it."

I think I can venture to believe that you do understand it all:—still I write, as he asked me. Perhaps you will kindly write me a few lines, which I may forward to him—to say that you understand his feelings. I feel sure that (if only for Hurrell's sake,) he would be pleased to have it done.

The dedication as it appeared read:

To

William Froude, Esq.

To you, my dear William, I dedicate these miscellaneous compositions, old and new, as to a true friend, dear to me in your own person, and in your family, and in the special claim which your brother Hurrell has upon my memory;— as one, who, amid unusual trials of friendship, has always been fair to me, never unkind;—as one, who has followed the long course of controversy, of which these Volumes are a result and record, with a large sympathy for those engaged in it, and a deep sense of the responsibilities of religious inquiry, and the sacredness of religious truth.

Whatever may be your judgment of portions of their contents, which are not always in agreement with each other, you will, I know, give them a ready welcome, when offered to your acceptance as the expression, such as it is, of the author's wish, in the best way he can, of connecting his name with yours.

I am, my dear William Froude,
Most affectionately yours,
August 1, 1871. John Henry Newman.

It was only when the book came to a second edition, within a very few months, that Newman learned of Froude's recent election to the Royal Society.

I am told [he wrote] William is F. R. S. I dare say he has a hundred letters besides, and I know nothing about it.

Will you tell me by return of post? for my book has come to a second edition, and I want to repair my fault and time presses.[13]

Throughout the years of correspondence one of the points over which Froude had experienced great difficulty was the infallibility of the Church, and his discussions had finally raised some doubts in his wife's mind. When the events leading up to 1870 brought forward prominently the question of infallibility, Mrs. Froude wrote to Newman asking him to explain the matter fully, and in replying Newman poured out with his customary frankness his view of the question, at the same time asking her to keep the letter since " I may want it. I have never before put my thoughts on paper."

[It] is a dangerous thing (he wrote) to go beyond the rule of tradition in such a matter. In the early times the Nicene Council gave rise to definitions and to confusions which lasted near a century. The Council of Ephesus opened a question which it took three centuries to settle. Well, these Councils were *necessary*—they were called to resist and condemn opposition to Our Lord's divinity—heresies. They could not be helped. But why is the Pope's infallibility to be defined?, even if denying it were a heresy, which no one says, how many do deny it? do they preach this denial? are they making converts to it, . . .

I am against the definition because it opens a long controversy—you can not settle the question by a word—whatever is passed, must be a half, a quarter measure. Archbishop Manning himself only aims at *condemning two propositions* i. e., at a *negative* act. How will that *decide* the question. No, it only opens it. At Nicea and Ephesus, great questions were opened, only opened, they had, as I have said, been opened by heretic priests. Now the Bishops of the Church

[13] Nov. 14, 1871. To Mrs. Froude.

are called upon to take the first step in opening a question as difficult, and not as justifiable, as the question which those early Councils were obliged to discuss. This question will lead to an alteration of the elementary *constitution* of the Church—Our one doctrine, in which all doctrines are concluded, is, " The Church's word is to be believed "—Hitherto " the Church's decision " means that of " the Pope and the Bishops "—now it is proposed to alter it for " the Pope's word." It is an alteration in the fundamental degree. Hitherto, I *personally* may be of the *opinion* that the Pope is infallible by himself *but I have never been called to act* upon it— no one has—and what is the consequence?, that the *Pope* cannot act upon it. Hitherto, the Pope has always acted, for greater caution, with the Bishops, he has not gone to the extent of what he might do, supposing him infallible. But, define his infallibility and he will act alone. Well, God will direct him—but what is this but throwing away one of the human means by which God directs him? It is making the system miraculous—and it is like seeking a bodily cure by miracle, the human means are [being] at hand.

I say, any decision will be a half or quarter measure—as the Councils of Ephesus and Chalcedon were such—it opens a very large question. Suppose you pass Dr. Manning's condemnation—still the positive question will be left open, and a new controversy will open, first what *is* the implied positive force of these negations?—let this be settled, then comes the question in *what matters* is the Pope infallible?—after this, when, under what conditions [?], is the Pope infallible? when e. g. he writes a letter? Councils are formal things, and there is no need of drawing the line between their acts, or not much need, but a Pope is a living man, ever living and it will be a great work to go through this question well. You have to treat it doctrinally—and then again historically, reconciling what you teach with the verdict of history.

Then again recollect that this doctrine is a retroactive doctrine, it brings up a great variety of questions about past acts of Popes, whether their decrees in past ages are infallible or whether they are not and which of them, and therefore whether they are binding on *us*.

If anything could throw religion into confusion, make sceptics, encourage scoffers, and throw back inquirers, it will be the definition of this doctrine. This I shall think even if it passes—because, though this doctrine must be inwardly received as true, its definition may be most unreasonable and unwise. I do not know that the Church is protected against inexpedient acts—though of course God overrules them—and also, when they are once passed, there is no good, and much disrespect and high-mindedness, in finding fault with them. Paul iii alienated England; I don't think he acted wisely; yet in one such [sense?] it was God's act because it was done.

Ever yours aff^{ly},
John H Newman.

P. S. Keep this; I may want it. I have never before put my thoughts on paper.

Questions of so great an importance were less frequently discussed in the few years now remaining. Newman's letters to the Froudes turned largely to reminiscences, light comment upon the topics of the day, and to an exchange of holiday greetings. Newman had now reached the pinnacle where he was to receive the fair guerdon of all his toil. Froude's work, too, was nearly finished, and, though he in no way ceased from his scientific investigations, he could not hope again to make the contributions of his earlier days. For eight years life moved on peacefully to an end which came suddenly.

In July, 1878, Mrs. Froude died. To Father Newman at the Oratory Froude at once dispatched a simple message:

Seven o'clock. She is just released after a long struggle

during which, however, she was quite unconscious, as we believe.

So severely did the loss of his wife bear upon him that Froude found it necessary to leave England for his health. He accepted the invitation of Her Majesty's Government to cruise to South Africa on the *Boadicea*.

As he set out upon his journey, Newman, too, was preparing to travel southward, to Rome, where he had been twice before, first as a prominent Anglican, then as a humble priest of the Roman faith. Now he was to return, as it were in triumph, to receive from Leo XIII the red hat, and to become a prince of the Roman Catholic Church. As he had done on the former occasion, Froude sent once again to Rome what were to be his final thoughts on those problems which had occupied the greatest minds of his time. It is not unfitting that these last speculations on metaphysics should have been set down on the blank pages of a pamphlet entitled " The Charter, Bye-Laws and Regulations of the Institute of Civil Engineers."

I have said that so far as I can see it is only out of the consciousness and sense of duty owed that we can rightfully construct the idea of a Divine *Person;* resting the opinion on the perception that the notion of a debt no less naturally involves the notion of the Person to whom it is owed than it involves the notion of him who owes it. The idea of a divine Person does not, to me, seem rightly to grow out of the perception of the existence of laws by which the course of nature is governed. I cannot feel that law implies a personal Lawgiver in the same way that debt implies a Person to whom the debt is owed e. g. I recollect that Bp. Butler expresses his belief that the Law of right and wrong is something which has a necessary existence " in the nature of things." Nor can I respond to Paley's dictum "whatever exhibits marks of design" etc. I recollect Hurrell pointing out, as if in anticipation of Darwin's view, that in many instances we can see plainly that what we call adaptations are consequences not causes, e. g. that the harder constitution of our ancestors who had a life of great exposure and hardship grew out of the fact that all weakly specimens were eliminated by those hardships.

Nor again can I build the idea of a Personal God out of the thoughts suggested by your paraphrase of the $\pi o\delta\lambda a$ $\tau a\delta\epsilon\iota\nu a$ in the Lyra.

"But oer the elements one hand alone has sway." I remember Hurrell saying in reference to this idea (though not in reference to the lines for it was long before they were written) that it would not startle him if we were to learn how to create a thunderstorm—in particular he expressed much contempt of the proposed Bridgwater Treatises—on the ground that the proposed "line of reasoning could not infer God except from phenomena not yet explained. It seems to me that working on this line of thought men are but like the image maker in Isaiah who made a God "of the residue thereof." But of course I quite feel that "granted a Creator" (do not suppose that I deny one) Infinite power and Infinite wisdom must belong to him, just as Infinite Righteousness must belong to Him to whom we owe it, each according to the talents given to us, to struggle to do right.

As regards the *traditionary* ideas of God and of our relation to Him, I must say there is much in them to which I feel that the law of right forbids allegiance.

In particular the idea that He is to be appeased by propitiatory sacrifice is a traditionary idea the very foundations of which seem to be open to our eyes in the present beliefs of savage nations; and it is one which when thus looked at and without the interposition of the profound theories which have been built up to justify it seem simply shocking and detestable.

The natives of the coast along which we are steering furnish a curious and striking instance of this which was new to me.

The surf along the coast and at the mouths of the rivers renders the upsetting of canoes a matter of frequent occurrence. This would have little terror for naked savages who swim like fishes, if it were not for the sharks with which the surf and the waves often swarm and by which when a canoe upsets every one of the crew is often devoured. So the shark, as a prime object of terror, is regarded as a God, is worshipped and has sacrifices offered to it. In the River Bonny especially it is considered a crime to kill a shark and to be eaten by one is considered as a road to heaven. There a shark is called Ju Ju. There is an order of priests to conduct the cultus and four times a year there is a Ju Ju festival and a sacrifice of goats, fowls etc. Mixing their own beliefs with the jabber of Christian oaths they have picked up from English sailors they say as a warning against shark killing "who kills Ju Ju him go dam, but who Ju Ju eat him go comantable" meaning that he will be comfortable in a future state. As late as 1840 openly, and secretly (it is believed) to a much later date, there was a yearly sacrifice of a young girl to Ju. Ju. The child was brought down yearly, quietly from the upper country and was carefully reared till she was about 10 kept without spot or blemish or scratch with the greatest care—in due time she was carried in a canoe on a plank stage to the mouth of the river under the pretence that she was being taken to her parents. Suddenly she was dropped into the river and in a moment devoured.

It may of course be said that this is merely a corrupted version of a Divine idea originally implanted in or communicated to our First Parents and I cannot prove that this is not so, but the assumption seems to me a forced one more suitable to one who argues $\theta\epsilon\tilde{\omega}\nu$ $\delta\iota\alpha\phi\upsilon\lambda\alpha\tau\tau\acute{o}\nu\tau\omega\nu$ than to one who seeks to know what is really true; and it is certainly interwoven with beliefs as to the origin of the human race which are year by year becoming more and more untenable, and I cannot but regard it as part of the natural fruit of these impulses which in animals no less than in man render the unknown a source of vague and subduing terror, and which in uninstructed men tends to frame the objects of the terror on the model of the things which are terrible here.

One at least of these things, and I think a characteristic one, is a capricious and tyrannical master whose favour can be gained by entreaty, cajolery or gifts, and this is one specially capable of having some shreds of the idea of " right " worked in with it as that idea grows.

Someone has recently said (well said it seems to me) : Man made God in his own image—but whoever it was that said it was anticipated by Isaiah . . .

I have only one thing more to say. Do not think that there is or has ever been since I began to think seriously a time when temptation has ceased to be a thing to be fought against or when if I have flinched from the battle or have failed to fight or have failed to win it has not been with lasting shame and self-reproach and with determination to renew the struggle more effectually; there is not and never has been a time when I have ceased to fear lest any repentance be inadequate.[14]

It was to answering Froude's last argument that Newman first turned his attention after his arrival in Rome. The long letter (quoted in Ward, *Life,* II, 586-92), a rough draft full of stylistic corrections, marks the end of a correspondence which extended through nearly half a century.

Rome
April 29, 1879.

I have been much touched by your consideration for me in writing to me, when you would put into shape your thoughts upon religion, thus putting me in your affection and regard, on a level with dear Hurrell; and I wish I had just now leisure enough and vigour of mind enough to answer your letter so thoroughly as I think it could be answered, and as its delicacy and tenderness for me deserves. But I will set down just as it strikes me on reading, having no books and depending mainly on my memory.

---

[14] Rough draft from among Froude's papers returned from South Africa.

My first and lasting impression is that in first principles we agree together more than you allow; and this is a difficulty in my meeting you, that I am not sure you know what I hold and what I don't; otherwise why should [you] insist so strongly on points which I maintain as strongly as you?

Thus you insist very strongly on knowledge mainly depending upon the experience of facts, as if I denied it; whereas, as a general truth and when experience is attainable, I hold it more fully than you. I say " more fully," because, whereas you hold that " to *select*, square, and to fit together materials which experience has supplied is the very function of the intellect," I should [not] allow the intellect to select, but only to estimate them.

I will set down dicta of mine, which I think you do not recollect, which are to be found in my University Sermons, Essay on Development of Doctrine, and Essay on Assent.

" No one can completely define things which exist externally to the mind, and which are known to him by experience."

" Our notions of things are never simply commensurate with the things themselves."

" It is as easy to create as to define."

" This distinction between inference and assent is exemplified even in mathematics."

"Argument is not always able to command our assent though it be demonstration."

" Concrete matter does not admit of demonstration."

" It is to me a perplexity that grave authors seem to enunciate as an intuitive truth, that everything must have a cause."

" The notion of causation is one of the first lessons which we learn from experience."

" Starting from experience, I call a cause an effective will."

" There are philosophers who teach an invariable uniformity in the laws of nature; I do not see on what ground of experience or reason they take up this position."

" Gravitation is not an experience any more than is the mythological doctrine of the presence of innumerable spirits in physical phenomena."

" Because we have made a successful analysis of some com-

WILLIAM FROUDE

plicated assemblage of phenomena, which experience has brought before us, in the visible scene of things, and have reduced them to a tolerable dependence on each other, we call the ultimate points of this analysis and the hypothetical facts in which the whole mass of phenomena is gathered up by the name of causes, whereas they are really only formulae under which these phenomena are conveniently represented" etc., and so on.

You say "I doubt whether it is really possible to give a blind man a common idea of a star." I have drawn out elaborately in one of my University Sermons the necessity of experience from the case of a blind man attempting to write upon colours, how he might go on swimmingly at first—but before long—in spite of his abstract knowledge would be precipitated into some desperate mistake.

I can't think you would write as you have written had you recollected in my volumes passages such as these. Therefore you must let me state what, according to my own view of the matter, I consider to be our fundamental difference, and it is certainly so considerable and accompanied with so [much that is] simply *a priori* and personal, that, if you really hold firmly
consider
all you say, I must with great grief (think) I shall have done all that I can do, when I have clearly stated what I conceive it to be.

We differ in our sense and our use of the word "certain." I use it of minds, you of propositions. I fully grant the uncertainty of all conclusions in your sense of the word, but I maintain that minds may in my sense be certain of conclusions which are uncertain in yours.

Thus, when you say that "no man of high scientific position but bears in mind that a residue of doubt attaches to the most thoroughly established scientific truths," I am glad at all times to learn of men of science, as of all men, but I did not require their help in this instance, since I have myself laid it down, as I had already quoted my words, [that] "concrete matter does not admit of demonstration." That is, in your sense of the word "doubt," viz. a recognition and judgment

that the proof is not wholly complete, attaches to all propositions; this I would maintain as well as you. But if you mean that the laws of the human mind do not command and force it to accept as true and to assent absolutely to propositions which are not logically demonstrated, this I think so great a paradox, that all the scientific philosophers in Europe would be unable by their united testimony to make me believe it. That Great Britain is an island is a geographical, scientific truth. Men of science are certain of it; they have in their intellects no doubt at all about it; they would hold and rightly that a residuum of defectiveness of proof attaches to it as a thesis; and, in consequence they would admit some great authority, who asserted that it was geographically joined to Norway, tho' a canal was cut across it, to give them his reasons, but they would listen without a particle of sympathy
as to
for the great man or doubt about his hallucination, and all this, while they allowed it had not been absolutely and fully proved impossible that he was right.

which

Then I go on to say, that [it is] just this, what scientific men believe of Great Britain, viz. that its insularity is an absolute truth, that we believe of the divinity of Christianity; and, as men of science nevertheless would give a respectful attention and a candid and careful though not a sympathetic hearing (to any man) of name and standing who proposes to prove to them that Great Britain is not an island, so we too, did men in whom we confide come to us stating their conviction that Christianity was not true, we should indeed feel drawn to such men as little as professors of science to the man who would persuade them that Great Britain was joined to the continent, but we should, if we acted rightly, do our utmost, as I have ever tried to do, in the case of unbelievers, to do justice to their arguments. Of course it may be said that I could not help being biassed, but that may be said of men of science too.

I hold, then, and I certainly do think that scientific philosophers must, if they are fair, confess too, that there are truths

of which they are certain, tho' they are not logically proved; which are to be as cordially accepted as if they were absolutely proved, which are to be accepted beyond their degree of probability, considered as conclusions from premisses. You yourself allow that there are cases in which we are forced and have a duty to act, as if what is but possible were certainly true, as in our precautions against fire; I go further so much, not as to say that in merely possible, or simply probable cases, but in particular cases of the highest probability, as in that of the insularity of Great Britain, it is a law of human intellect
the thought to accept with an inward assent as absolutely true, what is not yet demonstrated. We all observe this law; science may profess to ignore it; but men of science observe it every day of their lives, just as religious men observe it in their own province.

In opposition then to what you assume without proof, which you don't seem to know that I have denied, even to throwing down the gauntlet in denying, I maintain that an act of inference is distinct from an act of assent, and that [its] strength does not vary with the strength of the inference. A hundred and one eye witnesses add strength to the inference drawn from the evidence of a hundred, but not to the assent which that evidence creates. There is a faculty in the mind which I think I have called the inductive sense, which, when properly cultivated and used, answers to Aristotle's φρόνησις, its province being, not virtue, but the "inquisitio veri," which decides for us, beyond any technical rules, when, how, etc. to pass from inference to assent, and when and under what circumstances, etc. etc. not. You seem yourself to admit this faculty, when you speak of the intellect not only as adjusting, but as selecting the results of experience. Indeed I cannot understand how you hold certain opinions with such strength of conviction, as you[r] view of divine justice, of the inutility, if not worse, of prayer, ("it seems to me *impossible* that I should *ever* etc.) against eternal punishment, against the Atonement, unless you were acting by means of some mental faculty (rightly or wrongly used) which brought you on to assents far more absolute than could be reached by experience and the legitimate action of logic upon its results.

I am led to conclude then that you grant or rather hold two principles most important to my view of this great matter:—first that there is a mental faculty which reasons in a far higher way than that of merely measuring the force of conclusions by the force of premisses: and next, that the mind has a power of determining ethical questions, which serve as major premisses to syllogisms, without depending upon experience. And now I add a third, which is as important as any: the gradual process by which great conclusions are forced upon the mind, and the confidence of their correctness which the mind feels from the fact of that gradualness.

This too you feel as much as I should do. You say, "the communication of mind with mind cannot be effected by any purely abstract process." I consider, when I sum up the course of thought by which I am landed in Catholicity, that it consists in three propositions: that there has been or will be a Revelation; that Christianity is that Revelation; and that Catholicity is its legitimate expression; and that these propositions naturally strengthen the force of each. But this is only how I should sum up in order to give outsiders an idea of my line of argument, not as myself having been immediately convinced by abstract propositions. Nothing surely have I insisted on more earnestly in my Essay on Assent, than on the necessity of thoroughly subjecting abstract propositions to concrete. It is in the experience of daily life that the power of religion is learnt. You will say that deism or scepticism is learnt by that experience. Of course; but I am not arguing, but stating what I hold, which you seem to me not to know. And I repeat, it is not by syllogisms or other logical process that trustworthy conclusions are drawn, such as command our assent, but by that minute, continuous, experimental reasoning, which shows baldly on paper, but which drifts silently into an overwhelming cumulus of proof, and, when our start is true, brings us on to a true result. Thus it is that a man may be led on from scepticism, deism, methodism, anglicanism, into the Catholic Church, God being with him all through his changes, and a more and more irresistible assent to the divinity of the Catholic Church being wrought out by those various changes; and he will simply laugh and scoff at your doctrine that his evidence is necessarily defective and that scientific authorities are agreed that he can't be certain. And here I must digress a moment to give expression to a marvel that you should think I do not hold with [Hurrell]. "There is another point in which etc. etc. he used to feel that, whoever was heartily doing his best to do God's will, as far as he knew it, would be divinely guided to a clear knowledge of theological truth." Why, this is what I have enunciated or implied in all that I have written:—but to return.

You continue:—" The consciousness that they mean the same thing by the same words is a consciousness growing out of experience or daily experiment." This I have virtually insisted on in a whole chapter in my Essay on Assent, in which, among other instances in point, I refer to the difference of the aspects under which the letters of the alphabet present themselves to different minds, asking "which way does B look? to the right or to the left?" Moreover, it is the principle of my Essay on Doctrinal Development, and I consider it emphatically enforced in the history of the Catholic Schools. You must not forget that, though we maintain the fact of a Revelation as a first principle, as firmly as you can hold that nature has its laws, yet, when the matter of the Revelation [given] comes to be considered, very little is set down as the original doctrine which alone is *de fide*, and within which the revealed truth lies and is limited. As Newton's theory is the development of the laws of motion and the first principles of geometry, so the corpus of Catholic doctrine is the outcome of Apostolic preaching. That corpus is the slow working out of conclusions by means of meditation, prayer, analytical thought, argument, controversy, through a thousand minds, through eighteen centuries and the whole of Europe. There has been a continual process in operation of correction, refinement, adjustment, revision, enucleation, etc., and this from the earliest times, as recognised by Vincent of Lerins. The arguments by which the prerogatives of the Blessed Virgin are proved may be scorned as insufficient by mechanicians, but in fact they are beyond their comprehension, and I claim for theologians that equitable concession that they know their own business better than others do which you claim for mechanical philosophers. Cuique in arte sua credendum: I do not call your friends tho' "technical" in their mechanics, because you do call me "technical" in my theology; but I go so far as to take for my own friends what I grant to yours, and should ever do (so); I have long thought your great men in science to be open to the charge of superciliousness, and I will never indulge them in it. Our teaching, as well as yours, requires the preparation and exercise of long thought and of a thorough imbuing in religious ideas. Even were those ideas not true, still a long study would be necessary for understanding them; [when such a study is given] what you call the random reasonings of theologians will be found to have as clear a right to be treated with respect as those proceedings of mechanical philosophers who you say are so microscopic in their painstaking. Words are but the symbols of ideas, and the microscopic reasoner, who is not only so painstaking, but so justly successful in his mechanics, is simply an untaught child in questions of theology. Hence it is that we, as well as you, make such account of authority, even though it be not infallible. Athanasius, Gregory, Augustine, Leo, Thomas Aquinas, Suarez, Francis de Sales, Petavius, Lambertini, and a host besides have, from (our estimate of) their theological instinct that honour with us, which, on account of their mechanical and physical instincts, you accord to your men of material science. You say that an ordinary man would think it his duty to listen to any great mechanical philosopher who should bring reasons for even so great a paradox as the possibility of perpetual motion; why should such personal reverence be reserved for mechanicians alone? why not for theologians? To none indeed of the opinions

WILLIAM FROUDE

of the schools, nor to the reasonings even of Councils and Popes, are we bound; none are *de fide;* none but may be changed. I think there was a day when the whole body of divines was opposed to the doctrine of the Immaculate Conception; two great men, St. Bernard and St. Thomas, threw back the reception of it for 600 years. The Jesuits have reversed the long dominant opinion of St. Augustine of absolute predestination, and have been confirmed by two saints, St. Francis de Sales and St. Alfonso. On the other hand sometimes a doctrine of the schools has been made a dogma, that is, has been pronounced a portion of the original revelation, but this, when it has occurred, has been no sudden extempore procedure, but the issue of long examination and the controversy of centuries. There were circumstances in the mode of conducting the Vatican Council which I could not like, but its definition of the Pope's Infallibility was nothing short of the upshot of numberless historical facts looking that way, and of the multitudinous mind of theologians acting upon them.

What then you say of mechanical science, I say emphatically of theology, viz. that it " makes progress by being always alive to its own fundamental uncertainties." We may allowably argue, and do argue, against everything but what has been ruled to be Apostolic; we do (thus argue), and I grant sometimes with far less temper, and sometimes with far less freedom of mind than mechanical philosophers (argue) in their own province, and for a plain reason, because theology involves more questions which may be called burning than physics; but if you [who] are modest before Newton and Faraday may be fierce with table-turners, and the schola astronomicorum with that poor man who some years ago maintained

said that the moon did not rotate, I think it no harm to extend an indulgence towards the prejudicium or the odium theologicum, in religious writers.

And now I go on to the relation of the will to assent, in theological matters, as to which, perhaps from my own fault, I have not made my doctrine quite clear to you in the passage in Loss and Gain. You seem to think that I hold that in religion the will is simply to supersede the intellect, and that we are to force ourselves to believe against evidence, or at least in some way or other not to give the mind fair play in the question of accepting or rejecting Christianity. I will say then what I really meant. Now, as far as I recollect, Reding says, " I see the truth as tho' seen thro' clouds. I have real grounds for believing, and only floating imaginations against it; is this enough for faith? "

First of all, then, I had fancied that every one granted that in practical matters our wishes were apt to bias our judgments and decisions, how then is it strange that a Catholic Priest, as in that story, who was quite sure that there was but one truth and that he possessed it, should be urgent with a youth who was within grasp of this pearl of great price, lest, under the strong secular motives against his acting, he might through miss
faintheartedness lose it? But he would hold, and I hold most distinctly that, tho' faith is the result of will, itself ever follows intellectual judgment.

But again; it must be recollected, that since nothing concrete admits of demonstration, and there is always a residuum of imperfection in the proof, it is always also possible, perhaps even plausibly to resist a conclusion, even tho' it be one which all sensible men consider beyond question. Thus, in this day especially, new lights are thrown upon historical events and characters, sometimes important, sometimes, as the world agrees, clever, ingenious, but not likely to have a permament value. Now here it is the common sense, good judgment, φρόνησις, which sweeps away the aggressive theory. But there are cases in which judgment influences the will. Thus a tutor might say to his pupil, " I advise you not to begin your historical studies with Niebuhrism or you will end by knowing nothing; depend upon it the world is not mistaken in the grand outline of events. When objections come before you, consider them fairly, but don't begin with doubting," and his pupil might, by an act of the will, put from his mind, at least for the time, real difficulties.

Still more [does this apply] to the cases, not a few, in which excited, timid, narrow, feeble, or over-sensitive minds have their imaginations so affected by a one single difficulty connected with a received truth that [it] decides for them their rejection of it against reason, evidence, authority, and general reception. They cannot get over what so distresses them, and after a thousand arguments for the truth, return with full confidence to their objection. Thus if a man said he was fully convinced of the divinity of the Catholic Church, if he judged her by her rights, her doctrines, her history, or her fruits, but that he could not get over the fact that in the Apocalypse the dragon was red and red was the colour of the Cardinal's cassocks, I should (think) it would be the duty of a friend to tell him to put this difficulty aside by a vigorous act of the will, and to become a Catholic.

This is an extreme case; there are others more intelligible and to the point. Wives may be unfaithful, but Othello ought by a strong act of the will to have put aside his suspicions. Do you mean to say that a man can feel any doubt whatever of the truth and affection of an old friend? is he not in his inward heart fully confident and certain of him, while he will willingly own that there is a residue of doubt looking at the fact as a matter of inference and proof? Will it be anything to him that a stranger who has not his experience does not feel the force of them, when put into words? That stranger will of course disbelieve, but that is not reason against his own believing. You will say that cases of perfidy are possible, and a man may at length be obliged to pronounce against his friend; certainly, and (false) arguments may overcome the Christian and he may give up his faith, but, till such a strong conclusion has overtaken him, he will by an act of the will reject, it will be his duty, as well as his impulse to reject, all doubts, as a man rejects doubts about his friend's truth. And if it be said that his friend is visibly present, and the object of faith invisible, there the action of supernatural grace comes in, which I cannot enter upon here. It brings us into a leading question of premisses, not of proof. I have said much on this point in my Essay on Assent.

On the fourth of May, 1879, only a few days before Newman went to the residence of Cardinal Howard in Rome to receive formal notice of his elevation to the Cardinalate, William Froude died in Simon's Town, South Africa. Their last words spoken, they parted forever. The greatest of them moved forward yet further into certainty; the other, only less great, went forward too, but as he had always done—*incertus quo fata ferant, ubi sistere detur.*

The End.

APPENDIX

The following letters, unpublished hitherto, were written to William Froude by his older brother, Richard Hurrell Froude, in the years 1827 and 1828.

Oriel College, Oct. 28, 1827

My dear Willy

I have such a deal of business this term on my hands that I can hardly ever cribb a bit of time for writing letters. However I will not put off any longer thanking you for your long letter. I am very sorry to find that you are not on good terms with the other fellows in College, and though it is very possible, and indeed likely that the majority may in a case of that sort be in the wrong, still if it is only about amusements it is not worth while to set up for one's self on such trifles. There are quite enough serious matters on which a fellow may have opportunity to show his steadiness and how little he is influenced by the silly notions of others, and one ought to be glad of any trifling occasion of giving way, if it was only to show one's firmness on other matters was not obstinacy. I am giving you advice which I never used to follow myself, but now I try to do so as much as I can, having experienced the evil effects of a contrary conduct. If I was you I would try as much as I could to fall in with the general games, and even if it is a bore to be shinn'd at football, it is better than being disliked for shirking it. Besides it is no bad thing to be forced to bear pain now and then. So much for prose which I hope you will not set down as nonsense.

I have had dull week of it, since last Monday, but hope to get more in the way of it by and by. I think I shall make rather a good teacher of Mathematics, and am very glad you like them well enough to read them by yourself. If I was you I would skip the 4th and 5th Books, but read the 11th, also pay as much attention as ever you can to the Greek plays, both to the scholarship and construing, and then you will be able to start fair when you come here.

I had a very capital account of Bob the day before yesterday, stating that he had been down to Plymouth again and that Dr. Yonge had pronounced most favorably upon him. I believe he is still at Staverton enjoying his quarters.

You ask me I see about the mathematical way of finding the curve for a boat bows, now I fairly confess that I can not tell myself, but I know this much, that till you are very familiar with Algebra and Fluxions you have not the remotest chance of following the process; however, if you will get yourself Bland's Algebraical problems, and work a good many of the questions between this an Xmas I will undertake to bring you up to the point in the vacation.

I think I can explain to you the allusion Aunt Mary makes to Att's [1] promotion. For a day or two before I left home news was brought us that he had been put up into the class above him. I am afraid he is being pushed on beyond his age so much that it will make him stupid, for I am sure it is not a good thing for boys in general to live so much among fellows much older than themselves.

I am much gratified to hear that you are become such an expert sailor, but suspect that you spend too much time at it, and even on that ground recommend you to take to football; for you will have plenty of time to refresh your nautical dexterity before next Summer's expedition. My Father is really in earnest about building a cottage at Dartmouth. I think we ought to earn it by sticking to our work when away from home.

You are a very careless fellow about your money, and deserve to be taught its value by experiencing its want, but I will have compassion on you for this time, in consideration of the prose which I have taken on myself to inflict on you, forthwith I enclose 2 Bank of England Bills, and if they are not forthcoming send me word.

---

[1] James Anthony Froude, then fifteen.

I don't know whether I told you that I have a very comfortable set of rooms in College, and that their only defect is being up 2 pair of stairs. I suppose they will now be my permanent residence for a year or two, and I shall be able to accommodate you if it can not be contrived otherwise.

I will not bore you with an account of my daily labours, farther than that I have to give lectures to 3 successive classes from 10 till 1 one day, and from 11 till 2 the other, which lectures I have to learn before hand myself much more carefully than anyone who I am to teach need do, and that after next Tuesday I shall have to attend the Bp. of Oxford's lectures as a pupil myself, and besides this I have a private pupil of my own who has a right to demand an hour of me every evening, but this he has not yet exacted.

So that upon the whole I have as much on my hands as such a bad manager of time shall tell how to dispose of.

Good by

Your affectionate Brother

Rich H F.

Feb. 10, 1828.

My dear Willy

I was much obliged to you for your letter, and though I don't expect to be able to say much in return, I will try what I can do in the time I have . . .

I am very glad indeed to find that Westminster air is beginning to set you going again, and to help up the lee way you had made at home. I don't know that you can do anything more to the purpose than attend accurately to your school books at present, for if you make yourself a good scholar it makes very little matter how; and the Odyssey and Greek plays are as good a means of doing it as any, besides the advantage which you will have in a more immediate stimulous to read with accuracy.

I was surprised to hear you ever had any chance of Christ Church and give you great credit for saying so little of it. But however that turns out, if you are a sensible fellow, and look sharp after yourself, (I mean your weak points) you will get on very well. I am glad you stick at mathematics for it will be an immense lift to come here familiar with Euclid and Bland.

I have much less to get through this term than last, so I ought to do it rather better, though as yet I fancy I have not much succeeded. . . .

Yesterday I had very good fun in a long foot-barking expedition across country to beautiful places where I had never been before, one in particular where we had to cross a bog, jumping from tuft to tuft where ever there was a bit of solid ground with long grass on it. I had never been at the place before, and it seemed quite a different style of scenery from any thing one expects in such a civilized country.

In the evening I went to some wild beasts which had just arrived, and saw nearly the finest lion, in the largest cage, that I ever set eyes on. But there was such a set of blackguards there that to keep out of the crowd I was obliged to put up with a horrid place for seeing. Altogether yesterday was a great refreshment to me after the week's campaign and has set me on my legs again. Never mind sending me short letters as I shall be glad to hear from you whenever you have time to write, and particularly now, as you know by this time who will stay over. . . .

I heard a good account of Bob the other day.

> Good by
> > Your affec. brother
> > > Rich. H. F.

April 27, 1828.

My dear Willy

I will not delay to answer your letter though I fear I shall scarcely be able so to arrange and digest what I wish to say as [to] prevent my being in some things misunderstood. I am very glad to find that any thing has led you to think more seriously than you used to do of the necessity of exerting yourself and attending to the wishes of my Father, and feel no sort of doubt that if you do not suffer your present feelings to evaporate in talk (of which remember there is the greatest danger) you will probably recover the ground you have lost, and get rid of those selfish habits of which you seem now to be conscious. From the tone of your letter you seem evidently in great distress at the recollection of your past life. But I do not quite understand how far your self accusations extend, or whether you mean to intimate that you have acted contrary to what you think right in other respects than those in which we have always thought you deficient, and perhaps till I know something more about this I can hardly give you any useful advice. For you know one of the things with which we have always found fault, has been your great closeness about your pursuits, so that we are quite in the dark about you and hardly know you at all. But when I say this I do not mean that I wish you to disclose any of [the] bad thoughts or actions, which it might violate your feelings to repeat. I suppose everyone's conscience is distressed with enough of these, and you need not fancy them peculiar to yourself. But if your errors have been of a nature different from what I have had any reason hitherto to suspect, it might probably assist me in giving you advise, if you were to explain yourself a little more fully.

This then is the first thing which I wish to tell you; the next is that you must be habitually cautious of trusting any excited thoughts which Bob's death may have suggested to you. We are so constituted that emotions of this sort can last on our minds but a short time; and they are only intended to awaken us to exertion, not to produce permanent revolutions in our hearts. What you feel now may if you choose to make it so be the beginning of a real solid improvement in your character. But you must not imagine that the process can be a speedy one; and above all things must be cautious against getting into a way of speaking unnaturally.

I am now just come in from a walk which has kept me longer than I was aware, and shall be obliged to conclude without saying a good [deal] that I should have wished. But the two great things that I wish to impress upon you are the necessity of attending most closely to your conduct, and of putting very little confidence in your feelings. I do not at all press on you the expediency of relating to me any instances of past misconduct in yourself. But I think that it might be of service to you to have some friend aware of the sort of temptations to which you are subject, and depend upon it that nothing you can tell me will give me any right to despise you.

               Believe me my dear Willy
                  Your affectionate Brother   Rich H F.

                                      May 2, 1828

My dear Willy

. . . I am by this time less alert and up to my work than I was when I wrote to you a fortnight since, and hope you will excuse me if I make no amends for the uninteresting nature of my last communication. But by the by I will give you a hint that unless you can yourself get together a little more information than you did in your answer, you need not feel called on to write me so immediately. . .

By the by I wish some time when you have taken tolerable pains with a Latin verse exercise that you would take the trouble of writing it out for me in a letter. I should like very much to see the style of your exercises, as I fancy them a better test than most others of scholarship and mental refinement. And in this last respect, (as I hold a want of refinement to be one of your chief deficiencies) I should advise you to give them very especial care.

I have been reading the Georgics lately and they have rekindled my admiration for Virgil both as a Poet and a nice fellow, who only wanted instruction to make him a good religious man: and as far as I can see, Poetry and religion go so completely together, that without the last the first can be nothing better than humbug.

I happen to have very little time on hand just now and have to write home, which will occupy all the rest, so I must conclude with the information that I enclose you the sum of 3 £ which I hope will arrive safe.

By the by you need not annoy yourself at not being able to find words for Virgil, as it is a difficulty which you will find greater and greater, the more you get to understand his excellence. Only I would advise you to avoid the evil into which many fellows slip—of making this difficulty an excuse for construing slovenly. It would be as good a reason for carelessness in copying a beautiful drawing. For in both cases the dissatisfaction you must feel with your own performances is the great means of improvement.

You can not think what stupid vulgar fellows most of the men are with whom I am brought in contact here, and how impossible it is, to impress upon [them] the difference between good and bad in construing.

So hoping you will be a different cut from them

I remain   your affectionate Brother
Rich HF.

May 5, 1828

My dear Willy

I will not put off writing to you any longer, especially as the tone of your last letter was more what I could understand, than of that which preceded it.

No doubt the news of Bob's death must have been a great shock to you; and it is no wonder that being led by it first to think more seriously, you should have been a good deal excited and expressed yourself in an overstrained way. But as you now seem to be looking at things in their natural colours, I hope the resolutions which you form may be permanent, and lead to a great deal.

I was glad to find from you, that the censures which you laid on yourself in your last letter to me did not relate to any habits which you had formed without our being aware of it. For though in that case there might be more reason to rejoice in your being awakened, yet the task of overcoming yourself might have been much more difficult.

As it is, I hope that the habits of idleness, though they will long be a great annoyance to you, may be opposed by resolution, and the trouble and self-denial which this may take will strike at the root of selfish dumpy ways, more than any agitation of feeling which you may have experienced.

I am very much for having you decline Cambridge and come here as soon as I can get you a bed room in College, for I believe rooms will be out of the question. The best way will be for you to stay a few days in London after the Election is over; and in the meantime I should be able to arrange with the Provost so as to enable you to enter here, on your way home. It would be an advantage that you should enter the term before you come to reside, which you had best do after the Long vacation.

I am very glad you have been working quadratics, and don't think as far as Mathematics are concerned that you can employ your time to better advantage. For quickness is of much greater importance than you can now possibly suppose, and this can only be acquired by working many examples. As to Euclid you had better go into the 6th Book at once, and get up the earlier propositions, as you find them referred to. Take care however that you first understand the Definitions of the 5th Book, and work them by Algebra. . .

I suppose my Father has told you most of the circumstances of Bob's death, which I believe was more free from suffering than is usually the case. I look on the accident which made it happen while I was at home as one of the most fortunate that ever happened to me; though I fear I was able to be but of little use to him.

I have not time to say much more, except that I am very well and much better contented with my situation than I used to be.

> Good by my dear Willy
> and believe me your affectionate brother
>
> RHF

Heard from home today, they are now at Denbury for a little while, and all very well. I hope we shall get to know each other better in the course of time, and I should like often to hear from you how you are going on, and what you are doing.

INDEX

Apologia provita sua, 20; much read by men of science, 180.
Arian controversy, 45.

Bautain, Abbé, 30.

Chalcedon, council of, 44; unsettling nature of, 46-47.

Donatists, 47; parallel between Anglicans and, 48.

Froude, Anthony, 21.
Froude, E. M. (Isy — Baroness Anatole von Hügel), 109; letter from Newman to, 114.
Froude, Richard Hurrell, influence on William, 3, 22, 211; advice to William about studies, 213; moralizing, 215, 217; thinks Virgil a nice fellow, 216.
Froude, Mary, solicitude of Newman for, 109; only child who remained a Protestant, 109; death of, 153-54.
Froude, Richard Hurrell 2nd., conversion to Catholicism, 114; effect of conversion on education of, 143 *seq.*
Froude, Robert Edmund, 7; influence of Newman on, 148; conversion, 149; at Oratory school, 151; intention to enter priesthood, 154; confusion of ecclesiastical and religious state, 160 *seq.*; 167 *seq.*; doubts about Holy Sacraments, 181; later career and death, 172.
Froude, Robert Hurrell, Archdeacon of Totnes, 2; artistic accomplishments, 2; advice, 2.
Froude, Mrs. William, cast of mind, 11; questions Newman, 12; Roman sympathies of, 94; reception into Catholic Church of, 106; attitude toward Edmund's entering priesthood, 157-58; death of, 195.
Froude, William, youth, 3; Hurrell's influence on, 3, 9; inventions, 5; election to Royal Society, 6; death, 8, 210; influence on Newman, 8, 126; scepticism, 9; "sacred doubts", 9, 125; assistance to Newman, 11, in Achilli trial, 91-94; kindness to Newman, 16; attitude toward Newman's proselytizing, 16-17; reasons for corresponding with Newman, 18; tolerance, 19; suggests arguments to Newman, 20; urges Newman to write *Grammar of Assent*, 21; view of truth, 78-79; function of will, 78, 83, 135-136; view of private judgment, 85; view of Indulgences, 89; difficult medium of language, 97; estimate of wife's sympathy for Catholicism, 98; fear of effect of Catholicism on sons' minds, 109; criticism of Hurrell's reception, 116-124; debt to Newman, 117; desire for Newman's solution to problem of belief, 117, 129-30; different intellectual principles from Newman's, 118, 119-121; view of brother, Hurrell, 119; view of insight, 121-122, 126, 136, 181; influence of Butler's *Analogy* on, 124; criticism of faith, 122; concession to New-

man's argument, 126; criticism of Newman's argument, 135-38; objection to Edmund's entering priesthood, 162, 166; on Stephen's view of probability, 177; on probability, 180-181; declines Newman's offer of dedication, 185-87; tribute to Newman, 191; cruise to South Africa, 196; philosophical notion of debt, 196; on design, 197.

Grammar of Assent, 9.

Holdsworth, Miss Kate, 4.

Illative sense, 25; Froude's view of, 26-27, 28.

Keble, John, 3.

Lyell, Sir Charles, views similar to Froude's, 178; opinion of Newman, 180.

Monophysite controversy, 44.

Newman, John Henry, Cardinal, begins correspondence with Froudes, 11; state of mind in 1843, 12-14; approximating toward Rome, 12; slow progress, 13, 60; dissatisfaction with Established Church, 12; fear of unsettling William, 13-14, 50, 57, 63; reasons for writing to Froudes, 14-15; conversion, 15; as a proselytizer, 16; attitude toward Mrs. Froude, 17; sincerity, 17; asks Froude's assistance, 22; distinguishes two kinds of assent, 24; influence of Zeitgeist on, 30; encourages Mrs. Froude to write novel, 34; reliance on Froude, 35; in Achilli trial, 92-94; position in Anglican Church in 1833, 38; fears Roman trend of Anglican principles, 39; kept from Rome by repulsion, 39; violence against Rome, 39; contrast with Hurrell Froude, 40; obedience way to gain light, 41; reasons for his publishing, 42; confidence against Rome, 43-44; attempts to solve Froude's difficulty, 46; believes it right to resist doubts, 48; effects of Wiseman's article on, 48-49; corrects anti-Roman passages in writings, 49; view of corruptions, 49; reasons for writing Tract 90, 49-50, 62; view of Anglican argument, 52; on weakness of Anglican argument, 83; criticism of Anglican theory, 40, 53-57; how reconciled to modern portions of Roman system, 58-59; reasons for slow progress, 60; position in Catholic Church, 71; tone of correspondence with Froudes, 72-73; definition of faith, 77; duty to believe, 77, 78; argument from converts, 87; on Indulgences, 90-91; influence on Mrs. Froude, 95, 100-101, 103; reliance on Froude's philosophical argument, 99; solicitude for Froude children, 109, 111; explanation of Confession, 112; writes to Hurrell Froude 2nd, 112-13; reception of Hurrell into Catholic Church, 114-15; illative sense, 126; criticism of Froude's argument, 127-28; view of non-religious truth, 131; view of popular belief, 131-32; reliance on Froude's criticism, 132; disregard of degree of probability, 133;

INDEX 221

method of arriving at belief, 134; reliance on argument from authority, 134; on education of Hurrell, 143 *seq.*; on Edmund's conversion, 149-51; hope of converting Froude, 152-53; on Edmund's intention to enter priesthood, 155-56; doubts Edmund's vocation to priesthood, 158 *seq.*, 167 *seq.*; on Sacraments, 183; dedication of book to Froude, 185-92; on Papal infallibility, 193-95; final argument written to Froude, 199 *seq.*; differs from Froude on certainty, 201; on inductive sense, 203; propositions which led him to Catholicism, 204.

Palmer, Henry Robinson, 4.

Reed, Sir Edward James, 5.
Rogers, Frederick (Lord Blachford), opinion of Newman's thinking, 182.

Stephen, Fitzjames, article in *Fraser's* on "Dr. Newman's Apologia", 176; view of probability, 176.

Suffield, Fr., influence on Edmund Froude, 158, 161; leaves Catholic Church, 184.

Tract 90, reasons for Newman's writing, 49-50; unforseen opposition to, 50.

Vernunft, 23.
Verstand, 23.
Via Media, 45.

Wilberforce, Henry, attempts to convert Froude, 183.
Wiseman, Nicholas, article in *Dublin Review*, 47; influence on Newman, 48.

www.ingramcontent.com/pod-product-compliance
Lightning Source LLC
Chambersburg PA
CBHW060602230426
43670CB00011B/1937